Ritual and Remembrance
in the Ecuadorian Andes

Ritual and Remembrance
in the Ecuadorian Andes

RACHEL CORR

FIRST PEOPLES
New Directions in Indigenous Studies

The University of Arizona Press   Tucson

For Juan, Juanito, Alejandro, and Frank

The University of Arizona Press
© 2010 The Arizona Board of Regents

www.uapress.arizona.edu

Library of Congress Cataloging-in-Publication Data
Corr, Rachel.
    Ritual and remembrance in the Ecuadorian Andes / Rachel Corr.
        p. cm.
    Includes bibliographical references and index.
    ISBN 978-0-8165-2830-1 (cloth : alk. paper)
        1. Indians of South America — Ecuador — Salasaca — History. 2. Indians of South
    America — Ecuador — Salasaca — Rites and ceremonies. 3. Indians of South America —
    Ecuador — Salasaca — Religion. 4. Catholic Church — Ecuador — Salasaca — History.
    5. Fasts and feasts — Ecuador — Salasaca — History. 6. Salasaca (Ecuador) — History.
    7. Salasaca (Ecuador) — Religious life and customs. 8. Salasaca (Ecuador) — Social life
    and customs. I. Title.
        F3721.1.S28C67 2010
        986.15 — dc22   2009032147

Publication of this book was made possible, in part, with a grant from the
Andrew W. Mellon Foundation.

15 14 13 12 11 10   6 5 4 3 2 1

Contents

Illustrations

Preface

Ritual and Remembrance in the Ecuadorian Andes is a study of how the indigenous people of Salasaca have shaped and continue to shape their religion through ritual practices tied to the sacred landscape. I focus on two related aspects of Salasacan rituals: how Salasacans re-centered Catholic rituals to serve as mediums for sustaining indigenous cultural memory, and how people continuously re-create their religion through individual practice. In both collective and individual rituals, the landscape (mountains, hills, and pathways) is a central focal point for ritual action.

The study is based on eighteen years of intermittent fieldwork in Salasaca, an indigenous parish of twelve thousand Quichua-speaking people in the Andean province of Tungurahua, Ecuador. Many Salasacans opened their homes to me, taught me Quichua, included me in their daily and ritual activities, and spent long hours explaining their understandings of the rituals in which they participated. I am indebted to the people of Salasaca and regret that I cannot thank them all personally, but I would like to mention here some of the people who helped me the most over the years: Luis Anancolla; Andrés Pilla; Angelica Chagila; Patricio Caizabanda; Eduardo Chango; Zoila Culqi; Bernardo Jerez; Carlos María Jerez; César Jerez; Francisca Jerez; Rosa Jerez; Lidia Jiménez; Manuel Jiménez; Andrés Masaquiza; Augustina Masaquiza; Encarnación Masaquiza; Espirita Masaquiza; Gloria Masaquiza; José Masaquiza; José María Masaquiza; Manuel Masaquiza; Marcelino Masaquiza; Marcia, Noemi, and Samuel Masaquiza; María Masaquiza; Mariano Masaquiza; Pascual Masaquiza; Ramona Masaquiza; Rosa Masaquiza; Segundo and Jaime Masaquiza; Sixto Masaquiza; Zoila Masaquiza; Manuel Pandorga; José Antonio Masaquiza and Rosario Pambasho; and Dolores Sailema. For help finding historical materials on Salasaca I thank Elizabeth Fariño Vallejo; Carlos Luis Miranda Torres; Margarita Tufiño; Grecia Vasco de Escudero, director of the National Archive; Patricia Villalva Bermeo; and Wellington Yánez.

While living in Salasaca in 1991–92 I was fortunate to meet Norman and Sibby Whitten. In conversations in both Puyo and Salasaca, Norman and Sibby offered valuable advice to me even before Norman became my official mentor at the University of Illinois at Urbana-Champaign. I consider myself very fortunate to have had such a dedicated advisor as Norman Whitten. Norman and Sibby taught me the importance of undertaking careful fieldwork and to be attentive to Quichua linguistic expressions, kinship networks, and social relations while also considering how local people engage with national and transnational cultural systems. I also learned to discuss my anthropological interpretations and check my translations with indigenous consultants. I am indebted to the Whittens for their kindness, their hospitality in Ecuador, and their intellectual contributions.

While undertaking fieldwork in Ecuador over the years, I also benefited from conversations with and companionship from the Barrera Velasquez family, Kati Kaulbach, Eduardo Kohn and Mark Rogers, José Rivera, Deborah Truhan, Shed and Kris Waskosky, Tim Weaver, Lee Webb, and Peter Wogan. At the University of Illinois at Urbana-Champagne I was fortunate to have as my professors Janet Keller, Helaine Silverman, and Tom Turino. I am grateful to them for their constructive criticism and encouragement. For their friendship and comments on the early stages of this work, I thank Ann Denning, Michelle Johnson, and Michelle Wibbelsman. At Florida Atlantic University I received valuable advice from Jacqueline Fewkes, Michael Horswell, Tim Steigenga, Mark Tunick, and Dan White. I especially appreciate the extensive time Jacqueline spent patiently helping me with maps and figures. The photos that appear herein are all my own.

I gratefully acknowledge financial support from a Fulbright IIE grant, a Tinker Grant from UIUC, a Beckman Institute Grant (UIUC), a Fulbright-Hays Grant, a Research Initiation Award (Florida Atlantic University), a Faculty Development Award (Florida Atlantic University), and a Foundation Grant from the Wilkes Honors College. Parts of chapters 4 and 5 were published as articles in the *Journal of Latin American and Caribbean Anthropology* 2004 9(2):382–408; and 2008 13(1):2–21, and were adapted here with permission.

I thank Allyson Carter, editor-in-chief at the University of Arizona Press, for her help through the editorial process, and the two anonymous reviewers who carefully read and commented on the manuscript. Any shortcomings are my responsibility.

For helping me with child care during various stages of research, I wish to thank my parents, Grace and James Corr; my sister, Emily Corr; and my parents-in-law, Virginia Castro and the late Antonio González; Amalia Huanca; and my godchildren, María Manuela and Rosa Lucía Masaquiza. My husband, Juan González, has always been supportive of my continuing research. I dedicate this to him and to our children, Juan, Alejandro, and Frank.

Ritual and Remembrance
in the Ecuadorian Andes

CHAPTER 1

The Salasaca Runa

After the earthquake we went. I only remember a little bit, I was little. They said "Let's go [to the mountain Quinchi Urcu]. There we shall overcome this." Everyone went there to sleep at night, with fear. Everyone was crying, crying, asking God, praying, praying, praying. Many people from there, from here, from all parts, we all gathered together [*tandanacuganchi*].
—Marta Masaquiza, 1998

I was more than fifteen years old, so I remember well the experiences of the earthquake. . . . I was in the seminary of Quito, between the fourth and fifth course, but on the day of Friday, August 5, 1949, we had to go to Ambato to visit a cousin who was ill. . . . We were on our way back to Pelileo (by foot), because rumors were beginning to circulate that in Pelileo it had been the most tragic. . . . It was an impressionable scene to see one of the priests from Pelileo . . . and the nuns who had left Pelileo and were in Salasaca, they carried the Santísimo uphill, they had it in the plaza of Salasaca when we arrived, and Father Barros had to carry one of the nuns, I don't remember who it was, but she belonged to the community of Marianites. . . . In that earthquake five Marianites died in Pelileo, five priests and five seminarians died in the province of Tungurahua. We prayed to the Santísimo in the plaza of Salasaca and we went to Pelileo.
—Monsignor Vicente Cisneros Durán, former bishop of Ambato (cited in Miranda Torres 1994:122)

IN THE MEMORY OF THE YOUNG SEMINARIAN who would become bishop, he and other church ministers who happened to be in Salasaca at the time of the 1949 earthquake prayed in the plaza. In the wake of this frightening tragedy, the plaza, which marks the religious and civic center of Hispanic town layouts, was the locus of Catholic prayer. In the memories of an indigenous woman, Marta Masaquiza, her people turned to their sacred mountain following the tragedy. Throughout this book, I present the narratives of indigenous people who link historical memories and religious experiences, including early memories of Catholic catechism, to the sacred landscape. My goal is to show how one people, the indigenous Salasacans, shaped and continue to shape their religion through the performance of collective and individual rituals tied to the sacred landscape.

The Salasacans consider themselves to be a distinct ethnic group among Ecuador's indigenous peoples. They number around twelve thousand people, and their parish is located in the province of Tungurahua in the central Ecuadorian Andes. Like many highland Ecuadorian indigenous people, the Salasacans speak their native language, Quichua, and most Salasacans are bilingual in Quichua and Spanish. Salasacans proudly wear their distinctive ethnic attire: long wool, wraparound black skirts for women; long, black wool ponchos for men (see L. Miller 1998 for details). Like indigenous peoples throughout Latin America, Salasacans combine native Andean and Spanish-Catholic practices in their rituals. Modern-day ritual practices in Salasaca have been shaped by historical religious transformations and multicultural influences, including Andean mountain worship, Amazonian shamanism, and Spanish Catholic devotions to saints. This book shows how large-scale processes of religious change developed in a particular local, cultural context, and how indigenous people actively shaped and continue to shape their religion through ritual practice.[1] The study is guided by two related premises: (1) that indigenous religion emerged from historical processes and cultural encounters; and (2) that religion is meaningful insofar as it is experienced and understood by individual practitioners. These two related concerns guided my research, and the book is organized around this framework. While it is generally accepted in anthropology that indigenous cultures emerged through historical processes and cultural encounters, these processes must be understood as they developed in particular cultural contexts, just as religious rituals should be understood as they are experienced by individuals. This book analyzes Salasacan rituals by showing specific engagements with the Catholic Church and individual experiences with the sacred landscape. I will discuss theoretical approaches to ritual in the Andes later, but first it is necessary to provide some background information on Salasaca.

Salasacan Ethnohistory

Historians have outlined six cultural-linguistic regions for the pre-Columbian North Andes: the Pasto (northernmost region of Ecuador), Otavalo-Caranqui, Panzaleo, Puruhá, Cañar, and the Palta at the southern end (Newson 1995). The anthropologists Pieded Peñaherrera de Costales and Alfredo Costales Samaniego (1959:19–20) argued that Salasacans could be traced to the Panzaleo-Puruhá culture area of the central Ecuadorian Andes, based on their analysis of Salasacan surnames. The pre-Columbian North Andes consisted of independent chiefdoms and some confederations of chiefdoms in which commoners paid tribute to chiefs, and chiefs maintained power through management of trade to procure goods from different regions (Salomon 1986).

At the time of the Spanish conquest in 1532, the Incas were still in the process of fully incorporating North Andean chiefdoms into their empire. The Incas had varying degrees of influence in the North Andes, exercising greater control of the chiefdoms south of Quito and lesser control of the northern polities (Salomon 1986). One mechanism of imperial control was the practice of uprooting and transplanting populations, called *mitimaes*. Forced relocation served to place rebellious populations in regions that were already under control and loyal groups in areas that were resisting Inca imperialism. For example, many of the Cañar people of the southern Ecuadorian Andes were moved to Cuzco and other parts of the empire, while populations from the central and southern Andes were moved to the regions of Quito, Latacunga, and Saquisilí in Ecuador. Some of the ethnic groups north of Quito that battled against the Incas were relocated to Cuzco, the Lake Titicaca area, and other regions of the empire (Newson 1995).

The Incas offered benefits to cooperative chiefs and allowed them to rule over their ethnic territories while fulfilling administrative roles in the empire. After the Spanish conquest, native elites used ties with colonial officials to supersede ruling chiefs and usurp the chiefdoms (Powers 1995:157–67). These leaders, called *curacas* in Quechua and *caciques* by the Spanish, became administrators of tribute collection in their ethnic territories. Some caciques became quite powerful and ruled over several native groups (*parcialidades*). Each of these was headed by a "subchief" called a *principal*, who was in turn subject to the governing cacique.

The colonial Audiencia de Quito was organized into provinces, called *corregimientos*, governed by ruling hereditary caciques.

Many writings on the Salasacans state, ostensibly as a matter of fact, that the Salasacans were a population of mitimaes transplanted from Bolivia to their current location. To the best of my knowledge, however, no writer has cited documented evidence that the Salasacans were mitimaes. Colonial writers would explicitly mention the mitimae origins of other populations, such as the Guayacondo, Pomasqui, and Saquisilí (Newson 1995:360; Salomon 1986:161–67). Since it was common practice to specify mitimae populations in colonial records, the anthropologists Peñaherrera de Costales and Costales (1959) argue that the Salasacans were not mitimaes, citing the absence of such a designation in colonial documents. Among the Salasacans themselves, some embrace the claim that their ancestors originated in Bolivia, while others reject it (L. Miller 1998; Wogan 2004:24 n. 5).

My initial research into colonial sources on Salasaca revealed that many eighteenth-century Salasacans claimed to have migrated from the Sicchos-Collanas region (labeled Sigchos in fig. 1.1) of the Corregimiento of Latacunga.[2] Despite a major population decline in the early colonial period, the Latacunga region was considered one of the largest concentrations of indigenous people in the sixteenth-century Audiencia de Quito (Newson 1995:203). By the early seventeenth century, the Latacunga region was a major center of wool production for the textile industry, with much of the indigenous population forced into service as wool textile processors. Linda Newson (1995:223) estimates that by the beginning of the seventeenth century the indigenous population of the Latacunga-Ambato region was 28,840.

Within the Latacunga-Ambato region there were colonial indigenous migrations from Sigchos to Ambato (near modernday Salasaca), and the ancestors of some Salasacan families paid tribute to the native lords of the Latacunga region (ANE, Ind. 15-II-1712; ANE, Caz. 1-I-1728). In a case that lasted from 1710 to 1712, the cacique of "San Buenaventura de Salasaca," Don Francisco Masaquiza, claimed to be a subject of the governing cacique of Sigchos, Don Leonardo Hati. From 1699 until at least 1743, the tribute of these migrants to Salasaca went to the Corregimiento of Latacunga (Quishpe B. 1999:84; ANE, Ind. 9-III-1743). Some of the families who migrated to Salasaca had been subjects of an *encomienda*

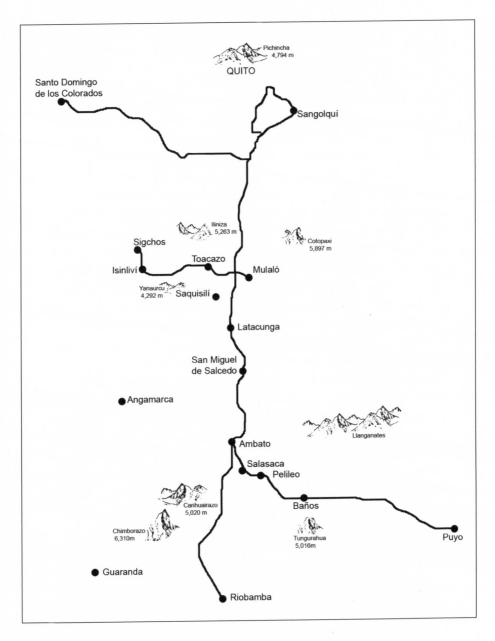

FIGURE 1.1. Map of the Latacunga-Ambato region. (Map by Jacqueline Fewkes)

(grant of indigenous labor) to an order of Spanish Bernadine nuns based in Madrid, to whom they paid tribute through their cacique, Don Francisco Hati Haja (ANE Caz. 1-I-1728).

Although much more research needs to be done, these initial findings indicate that Salasacan colonial history is one of migration and intermarriage, despite the homogenous ethnic identity of Salasacans in the twentieth century. Perhaps some of these colonial migrants were descendants of earlier mitimae populations, but we don't yet know. Many of the South American peoples who today exhibit strong cultural identities have their origins in colonial encounters (Hill 1996; Powers 1995; Schwartz and Salomon 1999;). As a people, however, Salasacans have maintained a strong sense of identity and cultural uniqueness, from their distinctive style of dress to their collective rituals and celebrations. Salasacans recognize other highland indigenous Ecuadorians, such as the Chibuleos, Saraguros, and Otavaleños, through each nationality's distinctive ethnic attire. Salasacans are comparable to the Saraguro people of the southern Ecuadorian Andes in that they were historically independent of haciendas and in their sense of ethnic pride (see Cassagrande 1981), but Salasaca is a much smaller community than Saraguro.[3] Outsiders have long been fascinated with Salasaca because of the perceived isolation, traditionalism, and "fierce" independence of the people (see Cassagrande 1981). The parish of Salasaca is surrounded by white (*blanco-mestizo*) towns. Although many Salasacans interact with their white neighbors on a daily basis, they proudly maintain the ethnic markers that set them apart: clothing, language, and cultural practices, including the rituals described in this book.

The Parish of Salasaca

When I started long-term fieldwork in 1991, the central plaza, located along the highway, was the site of the Catholic church, an elementary school, the high school, an artisans' cooperative, and the central post office, where the only phone in the community was located. There were a few family-owned convenience stores in the community, and a few *chola* vendors who sold food.[4] Many men had temporarily migrated over the years to work in construction and other jobs in the Galapagos Islands and coastal Ecuador, where there were more jobs and higher wages. Temporary, domestic migration to the coast and Galapagos Islands had been a part of Salasacan life for several generations, but few had traveled beyond Ecuador's borders.

By 1998 the community had changed dramatically. Many young people, both men and women, had migrated to France, Germany, Spain, and the United States. Entire families had moved to the Galapagos Islands, as opposed to the previous temporary migration of husbands and fathers. International migrants had sent money to their families for the construction of larger (two-story) cement block houses, and there were more paved roads. Money sent home by international migrants also allowed families to invest in small businesses in Salasaca.

When I returned for a visit in 2008, I found that several indigenous families owned restaurants, one owned a gas station, and one family was constructing a hotel for tourists. There were two Internet cafes and numerous businesses providing international phone calls, although most people had their own cell phones. People were proud to show me the community's new coliseum, where they could host concerts and other events. Salasaca is still mainly a rural community: all families have plots of land for their crops and raise some livestock, but now there are more conveniences available. For example, by 2002, many families had made DVD recordings of rituals and fiestas in which they participated.

Before Salasaca became its own parish in 1972, the people had to go to the town of Pelileo for all civil and religious functions. In ecclesiastical terms, Pelileo was the mother parish, and Salasaca was a rural annex. During the past three decades Salasacans have developed more civil and religious offices within their community, and Salasaca is now its own town. Salasacans have made increasing advances in regional and national politics as well. In 2008 the mayor of the (primarily white-mestizo) town of Pelileo was Dr. Manuel Caizabanda, an indigenous Salasacan and medical doctor.

Kinship and Social Organization

Most Salasacans live in nuclear family households, although extended families often live next door to each other. As the nuclear family grows, people may build additions on to their homes to make room for married adult children, or parents might allow a married adult child to live on a plot of land that they own.

From pre-Columbian times through the twentieth century, Andean societies have practiced trial marriage, in which a couple would live together for a year before formalizing their relationship as husband and wife (Price 1965). In Salasaca it is not uncommon for young adults to live together for years before having a formal marriage ceremony at the civil registry and then in the Catholic church. Some couples marry a year or two after they have a child together. Church weddings are big, expensive events, so the couple must work and save money in order to afford a formal wedding.

Salasacans extend their relationships to ritual kin. People choose godparents for Catholic sacraments such as baptism and sometimes confirmation. A young couple chooses an older couple to be matrimonial godparents for their Catholic church wedding. The older couple is supposed to act as built-in marriage counselors who intervene when the younger couple has marital problems. If the husband is at fault, the godfather could scold him or "pull on his ear" and the godmother could administer similar punishments to the wife if she is at fault. The nature of the intervention depends on the will of the godparents, and physical punishments were not common at the time I did fieldwork in the 1990s. One man told me that the godparents' home also served as a woman's shelter if her husband became abusive. Brides would be told that they should not return to their parents' home after getting married, but they could go to the godparents' home to escape an abusive husband. The godparents would then reprimand the husband and counsel the couple. This intervention is becoming less common as indigenous couples choose people from outside the community to serve as matrimonial godparents. I did however witness one incident in 1992 in which the elderly matrimonial godparents intervened, about fifteen years into the couple's marriage. A neighbor woman suggested to a man that his wife was being unfaithful. The man had been drinking that day, and he beat his wife. The wife's family quickly got word of the incident and informed her elderly grandmother, who then went and told the matrimonial godparents. The next day the godparents went to the homes of all involved and demanded that they go before the local (indigenous) lieutenant. According to local hearsay, the neighbor was charged a fine for stating something (the suggestion of adultery) of which she did not have direct knowledge, and the godparents counseled the husband on his abusive behavior, saying that he needed to control his jealousy. The case illustrates how the godparent bond formed through the wedding ritual fifteen years earlier served to guide the couple through the dispute.

The indigenous practice of *compadrazgo*, or ritual co-parenthood, is a well-known example of how indigenous people use colonial Spanish Catholic institutions to their own ends (Lyons 2006:83–85; Mintz and Wolf 1950) and interpret ritual kin relationships in terms of indigenous social relations (Uzendoski 2005:106–7; N. Whitten 1976:139). When a couple serves as godparents to a child, they become "co-parents" with the child's parents. This relationship between couples can strengthen existing relations of kinship or friendship, or it can serve as a way for a family to extend their network of social relations.

In addition to forming ritual kin through Catholic sacraments such as baptisms and weddings, people throughout the Andes choose ritual godparents for other occasions, such as the child's first haircut. In the southern Ecuadorian Andes, the person who cuts the baby's umbilical cord becomes a type of godparent (Brownrigg 1977). Salasacans have created a category of ritual kin called *saruc* ("one who set his/her foot down"). The saruc "mother" or "father" is the first person to come to the home after a baby has been born, without knowing that a birth has taken place. Many Salasacan women give birth at home, and births are quiet, intimate affairs that are not publicly announced. It is not uncommon for someone to come to a neighbor's home, to borrow a tool, for example, or to invite someone to accompany her to the market, without knowing that a baby was born the night before. The family will then say "Saruc Mama!" if the person is a woman, or "Saruc Tayta!" if it is a man. Once the relationship is declared, it is up to the individual will of the adult to buy occasional gifts for the "saruc child" if he or she wishes, as in the following event I witnessed while visiting my friend Carmenza in 2002.

One day, early in the morning during the feast-day celebrations of Corpus Christi, a man came by Carmenza's house holding two live chickens, one male and one female (Qu. *cari-huarmi*). He appeared to have been drinking during the festivities. He was looking for Carmenza's nineteen-year-old daughter. When she came out of the house, the man gave her the two chickens and left. Carmenza explained that the man was her daughter's saruc tayta. I wondered why he was giving her a gift at this time, seemingly out of the blue. "What's the occasion?" I asked. "There's no occasion," Carmenza explained. "Upon remembering (*yuyarisha*), one brings a gift." I then recalled that when Carmenza's nephew was little he owned a white dove given to him by his saruc tayta. On another occasion I was with a woman at the market when she remembered her saruc daughter and decided to buy a dress for the child.

The saruc relationship differs from sacramental godparenthood in that it is not planned or selected but is based on a serendipitous event. It nevertheless creates a new social bond between the child and the (outsider) adult who sets foot in the house after the birth. In Carmenza's case, nineteen years after the birth of her daughter, the saruc tayta still remembered the relationship and came to give a gift to the young woman. The wife of the saruc tayta also gave Carmenza's daughter a red shawl and promised to give her two pigs if she would help her with some chores around the house, but the daughter didn't have time because she was too busy with schoolwork. Carmenza described her daughter's relationship with her saruc tayta:

> I was lying in bed the morning after giving birth, and he came by the house to ask my husband to go with him to get firewood. When the saruc tayta is the first person to set foot in the house for a baby girl, the girl's heart develops like his. My daughter is hot-tempered just like her saruc tayta, and a baby boy's character comes out like his saruc mama's.

For Carmenza, if the fictive kin relationship is a cross-gender one, it affects the disposition of the child (see also Jerez Caisabanda 2001:55). One's saruc parent is also mentioned in the list of names of relatives who are announced at the death of a person in the community, showing that he or she is considered kin.

Political Organization and Collective Labor

Since 1972 Salasaca has been an independent parish with an indigenous *teniente político*, a local lieutenant elected by the Salasacans and officially appointed by the Ecuadorian Ministry of Government. The town council (Sp. *junta parroquial*) organizes meetings about community-wide affairs and represents the community to outsiders. The president of the junta parroquial is elected by the people and is the highest authority in the community. From 2004 to 2008 this position was held by a woman with a college degree.

There are several bilingual schools, one high school, and an experimental school started by indigenous people as an alternative to the state- and church-run schools. Some parents choose to send their children to high schools in the nearby towns of Pelileo or Ambato.

Beyond the local community, Salasacans serve as representatives on national indigenous rights organizations such as the provincial-level organization MIT (Indigenous Movement of Tungurahua) and the national-level CONAIE (Confederation of Indigenous Nationalities of Ecuador). Through these organizations Salasacan people partake in dialogue with other indigenous leaders to protect their rights and promote their interests in Ecuador.

Each of the eighteen hamlets that comprise the parish of Salasaca is headed by a number of men and women called *cabecillas*. The cabecillas are responsible for organizing nightly patrols to prevent theft. They also organize political meetings, called *juntas*, and take attendance at *mingas*. Mingas are the communal work projects for building roads and meetinghouses, cleaning canals, and caring for the cemetery. This important institution is a pervasive part of life in Salasaca and deserves some attention.

One representative from each household is required to attend each minga, and if a household is not represented, the cabecillas come to the house to charge a fine. The money is used to purchase drinks for the other minga workers. The cooperative, egalitarian nature of the minga is further demonstrated by another rule. Very rarely, mingas have turned tragic, leading to deadly landslides in which people have been killed. My *comadre* Anita explained to me that when a person dies during a minga, the other minga workers are responsible for paying for the funeral, and they serve as pallbearers.

A typical day in Salasaca starts out with early-morning announcements over the loudspeakers stationed in each sector of the community. One man is in charge of making announcements, and people bring their requests to him in order to disperse information throughout the parish. He begins each morning with the greeting "Good morning, people of the Parish of Salasaca," then proceeds to read a list of announcements for the day. For example: "Listen up, parents of schoolchildren. There will be a meeting at the high school today at 3:00 sharp. You *must* be there. Any parent with a school-age child who does not show up will be charged a fine. And, for those of you who have land in sector X, there will be a minga today at 9 a.m. sharp, to build an irrigation ditch. Bring your shovels and a *cocaya* (sack lunch). Every person who has land in this sector must send a representative or pay a fine. . . ." And as the day goes on, new announcements are made.

The minga, a pre-Columbian form of collective labor, is the way by which rural people in Ecuador maintain their communities. If a household is required to participate in a meeting or minga, the members decide which person will represent the family there. Each cabecilla has a list of names for his or her sector, which is checked off at the minga. One morning, Anita was at home, serving a breakfast of potato soup to her children, who were getting ready for school. Her husband had already left for a local construction job at which he was temporarily employed. As she listened to the announcements being shouted over the loudspeaker, she sighed. "We have land in that sector, but I have another meeting I have to go to today. What am I going to do?" Her thirteen-year-old daughter said, "I'll go to the minga, Mama." Anita ignored the offer. "If I don't go to the meeting, they'll charge a fine, and if I don't go to the minga, they'll charge a fine." Again her daughter offered, and was ignored. Then I added, "Comadre, just go to the meeting and I'll pay the fine for you. What else can you do?" She ignored my offer as well. Her daughter again pleaded, "Please, Mama, send me to the minga." Finally, Anita gave in to her daughter: "All right, but they'll give a test, a heavy stone to carry, for example, to see if you are strong enough. And don't goof off with the other young people; you just focus on the work." As the daughter prepared to leave for the minga, where she would be joining her teenaged cousins and friends, I asked Anita quietly, "Will she be able to do it? Won't they fine you for sending a kid to the minga?" Anita replied, "Oh, she's strong enough all right. The problem with sending adolescents to mingas isn't that they are physically incapable of the work, it's that they get distracted and play with each other instead of focusing on the work." Thus began the daughter's role of representing her household at mingas when the parents were busy with other tasks.

Studying Andean Ritual

I did not originally set out to study ritual in Salasaca. After a brief period of fieldwork in 1990, I returned to Salasaca in 1991 for a year, with the goal of studying child socialization. During this time I participated in many daily activities with my host family (Anita, Mariano, and their children) and others. I slowly began to learn Salasacan Quichua through daily practice, and Salasacan women taught me how to spin wool by hand. Although I had set out to study child socialization, I realized I was learning more and more about Salasacan uses of sacred places on the landscape, especially mountains and crossroads. As people told of a supernatural experience, they always mentioned where it happened: for example, which rock someone had passed before becoming ill. I accompanied several different people to leave offerings at sacred places, and on several occasions I accompanied a local shaman when he went to pray and leave offerings at mountain shrines. I attended the curing sessions of several different shamans, who served both Salasacans and blanco-mestizo clients who came to the community to be healed. During subsequent summer trips to Salasaca in 1993 and 1996, I continued to participate in Salasacan daily activities as well as sacred rituals, and by then I could conduct in-depth interviews and collect oral histories in Quichua, rather than Spanish. However, I always clarified certain parts of the recorded interviews with Salasacan consultants who were Quichua-Spanish bilinguals. This enabled me to get a better understanding of some of the meanings implicit in certain Quichua expressions.

I went to live in Salasaca again in 1997–1998, this time to undertake research on Salasacan religious experiences with sacred places. At that time, however, there was an anthropological shift away from a focus on local rituals and symbolism. One reason for this was a general trend in anthropology away from local case studies in favor of a focus on globalization (see the discussion in Abercrombie 1998a). In the Andes, the anthropological critique of studies of local-level symbolism focused on the "failure" of anthropologists working in Peru to foresee a violent upheaval brought on by the guerrilla movement Shining Path and the military's brutal response to it. Andeanists argued that the emphasis on indigenous communities as bounded, isolated entities, and the focus on local-level rituals "blinded" anthropologists to the growing political unrest around them (Isbell 1985:xiii–xiv; Starn 1991, 1994).

Furthermore, scholars of Latin American indigenous religion in the 1990s criticized two tendencies in anthropological studies. One criticism was that there was a polar tendency to portray indigenous peoples as either passive victims whose culture has been destroyed by colonialism, or resistant bearers of their ancient heritage under a thin cover of Christianity (Abercrombie 1998b; Griffiths 1999; W. Taylor 1996). This problem is not insurmountable. One can avoid falling into such extremes by focusing on historical processes, agency, and individual meanings of cosmological concepts. Therefore, my study of Salasacan ritual includes analysis of both historical interactions of indigenous people with agents of the Catholic Church, and of the meanings of rituals to individual actors today. While many earlier ethnographic studies of Andean cultures have been criticized for focusing on the persistence of pre-Columbian ways, recent works are more concerned with colonial history, power, and recent social and political changes.[5] Anthropologists now accept that indigenous religion represents neither a pre-Columbian continuity nor a colonial imposition. In fact, some of the rituals and symbols that most prominently express indigenous collective identity developed on the colonial frontier of Iberian Catholic and native Andean cultural contact (Abercrombie 1998b:114–15; Rappaport 1994:95). Although this cultural frontier was marked by asymmetrical power relations, indigenous peoples used Spanish Catholic institutions to maintain indigenous identities. I situated my study of Salasacan rituals within the theoretical frameworks that developed from criticisms of earlier ethnographies. In my research, however, I aimed to move beyond general descriptions of rituals and spiritual entities, such as mountain spirits, saints, and shamans, to include a focus on individual practices.

The Landscape and Lived Religion

There are many excellent studies of both Andean ritual and the significance of sacred mountains in the Andes, though most of these focus on Peru and Bolivia (Abercrombie 1998b; Allen 1988; Bastien 1978; Harvey 1997; Isbell 1985; Sallnow 1987; but see Rappaport 1998 and Wibbelsman 2009 for North Andean studies). For example, in her analysis of coca and cultural identity among the people of Sonqo, Peru, Catherine Allen (1988) shows how the reciprocal sharing of coca leaves mediates human social relations with each other and with mountain spirits. Coca chewing is not practiced among Ecuadorian indigenous people today, but indigenous Ecuadorians have their own ways of mediating relationships with the human and the divine through ritual. This study of Andean ritual offers both a North Andean focus and an emphasis on a variety of individual practices. In my research I endeavored to understand the exact nature of people's use of sacred places. What does it mean to say that people "believe in" sacred places? To answer this I interviewed many different individuals during my fieldwork, and I focused not only on what people said, but on what they did; that is, the nature of ritual practice as lived religion (Orsi 2002:xix–xxiv).

Several anthropologists have analyzed the interaction between individual experience and collective symbols and cultural patterns (Abu-Lughod 1991; Dougherty and Fernandez 1981; Fernandez 1965; Firth 1973; Gottlieb 1992; Stromberg 1981). These studies are crucial to our understanding of how individuals transmit, re-create, or change cultural patterns. When a shaman, as a ritual specialist, summons mountain spirits, do his clients share his understanding of the ritual? Does it reflect a shared cosmology or the personal views of the shaman? These questions guided my research over the years, and I present multiple, individual Salasacan explanations of their own ritual practices. I do not favor anthropological analysis over indigenous explanations, and I do not view interpretive analysis as precluding indigenous explanations. Andeans themselves have expressed the awareness that rituals have more than one meaning (Turino 1993:98), as well as the wisdom that "we can't know everything." I often discussed my anthropological interpretations of symbolism with Salasacans. Sometimes they said I was right and offered details to support my explanations, sometimes they said I was wrong and corrected me, and sometimes they said, "We've never talked about it like that, but you could interpret it that way." This ethnography emerged from the fieldwork, and while I offer my own interpretations and analysis, whenever possible I prefer to present indigenous explanations for their own rituals and experiences. Such explanations may not be satisfactory to anthropologists who are searching for grand theories: they are often as simple as "we do it because it works," or "we do it because that's what our ancestors did." With such explanations,

I try to suggest interpretations without imposing on indigenous views of their own practices.

In my focus on ritual in historical context, I compare some elements of ritual practice to pre-Columbian and early colonial practices. A study of historical change in rituals does not preclude attention to such pre-Columbian continuities: to the contrary, it is a necessary component of such a study. Furthermore, indigenous people are proud that they maintain many aspects of their ancestors' rituals. However, many traditional religious and cultural practices of indigenous Latin Americans have Iberian roots, as George Foster cautioned in his 1960 book *Culture and Conquest* (see also W. Taylor 1996). It is not always possible to distinguish pre-Columbian from Iberian-derived practices, and such a detangling of origins is not my goal, but I do make reference to pre-Columbian precursors of some rituals.

Although there are a small number of Protestants in Salasaca, Protestantism has not taken a strong hold there. The first North American Protestant missionary came to Salasaca in 1945, and today there is an indigenous-run Protestant church. Protestants in Salasaca (called *evangélicos*) abstain from drinking alcoholic beverages, dancing at sacred places such as crossroads, and honoring Catholic saints. They do however strive to maintain as many cultural traditions as possible without violating their religious beliefs. For example, some Protestants make unfermented maize beer for weddings. Others play traditional Salasacan music. While I do not deny the existence of Protestants in the community, my analysis of Salasacan rituals addresses only non-Protestants. Furthermore, unlike other indigenous people in the Andes, Salasacans have not been profoundly influenced by post–Vatican II approaches to Catholic theology such as liberation theology (Lyons 2006) and inculturationist theology (Orta 2004), so I do not discuss these changes in Catholic teachings, which have affected other Latin American indigenous societies. Rather, I show the negotiations between the church and indigenous rites that occurred in the late nineteenth and early twentieth centuries, as Salasacans selected and manipulated aspects of Catholic discourse and ritual, and priests attempted to compromise with indigenous people.

Finally, I should add that I have chosen to focus on religious rituals in this book just as other studies have focused on gender, economics, or political activism. The rituals and beliefs I present here are extracted from years of fieldwork in 1991–92, 1993, 1996, 1997–98, 2002, 2004, 2005, 2006, 2007, and 2008. On a daily basis, of course, Salasacans are concerned with many of the same issues as many other people: how to afford their children's education, whether to migrate to a foreign country for work, who to vote for in the next presidential election, or whether to invest in buying a pickup truck. Ritual is just the one of many aspects of their lives on which I have chosen to focus. This may seem obvious, but I am sensitive to the fact that a focus on religious ritual runs the risk of portraying people as "mystical" in a way that denies their participation in modern national and global events.

Outline of This Book

This book is divided into two parts. The chapters in part I (chaps. 2, 3, 4, and 5) focus on how Salasacans shaped colonial Catholic rituals and texts to serve as mediums for sustaining indigenous cultural memory. Participants in collective rituals use the techniques of re-centering texts, tracing out local sacred pathways, and ritual intertextuality in order to sustain Salasacan collective memory. I illustrate these strategies through collective rituals of ceremonial blessings, placemaking ceremonies, mimesis and parody of Catholic rituals, and commemorative death rites. The chapters in part II (chaps. 6, 7, and 8) show how individuals experience the historical-religious transformations discussed in part I, and how people continually sustain and re-create religion through private ritual practices, with a focus on consultation with shamans, prayers, and offerings to mountain spirits. Together the two parts show how indigenous people have been and continue to be active in shaping, sustaining, and re-creating religion.

Both collective and individual experiences are organized according to the sacred landscape, especially ritual pathways, mountains, and crossroads. The place that is most salient in practice is the crossroads called Cruz Pamba, where several roads merge into two roads that meet and become one road leading to the town of Pelileo. The place where the roads meet has been sacred for generations, and there is a hole in the ground where people leave offerings. In 1994, the *alcaldes* (officers responsible for sponsoring fiestas) dedicated a large stone cross to the community and placed it at the spot where the roads meet, leaving space at the base

FIGURE 1.2.   Cruz Pamba, a sacred crossroads leading into Pelileo.

of the cross for the hole underground (see fig. 1.2). A series of connected
sacred hills rises up from Cruz Pamba. These are Catitagua, Quinchi
Urcu, and Palama (the shrine at Palama is also called Nitón Cruz). These
mountains have holes and crevices at the top where people leave offerings
and pray. Throughout the 1990s, I visited the shrine on Quinchi Urcu
where *achupalla* plants covered an opening at the top of the hill. In 2002,
a large wooden cross had been placed there by a mestiza woman, although
mestizos don't typically leave offerings at Salasacan sacred places. When
I asked about the cross, Salasacans said that a woman from the town of
Pamatuc placed it there. According to the story, the woman heard that
Quinchi Urcu was a good spot to pray. She had some (unknown) illness
but recovered after leaving an offering at the shrine. After she was healed,
she went with a priest to place a large cross at the spot. Salasacans continue
to leave offerings there, as they always have. Because the landscape is such
a pervasive part of ongoing religious practice in Salasaca, these places
will be mentioned frequently throughout the book; consult figure 1.3 for
orientation. In addition to the crossroads at Cruz Pamba and the series of
mountains rising up from Cruz Pamba, the map in figure 1.3 shows the
original center of Salasaca, Chilcapamba (spelled Chilka Pamba on the

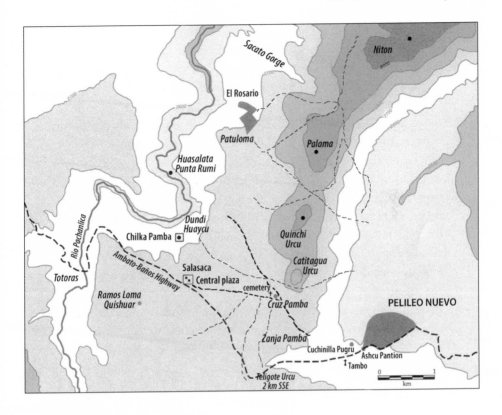

Figure 1.3. Map of Salasacan sacred places.

map). San Buenaventura, the patron saint of Salasaca, is still housed in the old chapel there (for this reason it is also referred to as Capillapamba).

In the following chapter I provide a historical background to Salasacan ritual life. After a brief general discussion of colonial religious practices, I focus mainly on the early twentieth century. I discuss indigenous interactions with the Catholic clergy, the incorporation of Catholic symbols into Andean religious practices and, in chapter 3, the development of indigenous social roles based on church activities. The office of festival sponsors became a significant part of indigenous culture, and in chapter 4 I show how the alcaldes have maintained Salasacan cultural identity through Quichua prayers and ritual circumambulations in the community. The colonial Catholic institution of festival sponsorship has become a means of sustaining indigenous cultural memory through oral texts and through movement along ritual pathways. I continue to explore the theme of Salasacan memory practices in chapter 5, where I focus on mortuary customs and kinship. I explore the meanings of sacred play and the parody of the Catholic mass conducted in order to perform a ritual transformation at death. Salasacans use ritual intertextuality to incorporate parts of one ritual into another and in this way combine ritual elements from the Catholic mass into indigenous mortuary and memory practices.

In part II of the book I move beyond an analysis of collective rituals to focus on how individual actors experience ritual. Chapter 6 focuses on the "moral topography" of Ecuador. Throughout Ecuador, the Amazonian tropical forest is viewed as the locus of strong shamanic powers, in contrast to the church-state controlled power of "civilized" society. I present the personal narratives of Salasacans who have been healed by Amazonian shamans, including one healed in a session that took place during the 1992 political march to the nation's capital. I analyze these healing narratives in historical-geographical context. In chapter 7 I focus on Salasacan shamans, who have contact and training from both highland and Amazonian shamans, and who use local sacred places to heal both indigenous and white clients. I present the chants of a shaman who names both powerful mountains of the Andes and lowland regions of Ecuador, in order to heal his clients, and I analyze a shaman's Quichua prayer to the mountain mother as he leaves offerings. Chapter 8 presents individual religious experiences and shows that sacred mountains and crossroads in Salasaca are part of lived religion. While Salasacan culture cannot be understood apart from the history of Catholic indoctrination, practices such as mountain worship continue despite colonial church efforts to stop "idolatrous" practices. Through an approach that Lila Abu-Lughod (1991:153) calls "ethnographies of the particular," I focus on the individual meanings of cultural practices. Together, the chapters show how indigenous people make use of intertextuality, narrative, and ritual movement both to solve personal problems (related to illness, love, or being a productive person) and to maintain a sense of collective memory and identity.

In order to illustrate the complexities of life for Salasacans in modern Ecuador, I weave excerpts from my recordings of conversations and events I witnessed over the years throughout the text. These excerpts illustrate what I perceived from social interactions, jokes, arguments, resolutions, and everyday life experiences of the people I lived with. Although I try to avoid becoming overly reflexive, I occasionally present stories of how I came to learn about certain Salasacan values. After all, it is often through blunders, mishaps, or other spontaneous events that an anthropologist learns the underlying meanings and values of cultural institutions such as kinship, reciprocity, age hierarchies, and social relationships.[6]

In writing Quichua words, I have chosen not to use *w* and *k* in most places, because most Quichua speakers I know do not use these spellings. For words that could be spelled with *w* I use *hua* or *gua*, as in the words *huasi* (*wasi*) and *guagua* (*wawa*). The *j* at the beginning of a word is pronounced like the English *h*, but at the end of a word it is pronounced like a hard *g*, as in *rezachij* (*rezachig* or *rezachic*). I use the *j* here to mark the agentive case, following Kristine Waskosky (1992). When discussing general characteristics of the language, I use the term *Quechua*, the family of languages to which Quichua belongs. Unless otherwise noted, all translations from Spanish are my own, with the assistance of Juan González.

I spent time in the homes of different Salasacan families and interviewed many different people. I use pseudonyms throughout the book to protect people's privacy, but those Salasacans who appear in photographs gave me permission to use their real names.

PART I

Collective Rituals and Memory

CHAPTER 2

The Catechist and the Quishuar Tree

Religious Transculturation in the Andean Contact Zone

INDIGENOUS CULTURE TODAY is the result of cultural encounters and historical processes, but the trajectory of those processes must be understood locally. In this chapter I show how the colonial religious projects of Spain and the indoctrination policies of the Catholic Church after independence affected indigenous society at the local level. The official instructions regarding sacraments, preaching, extirpation of idolatries, and indoctrination had far-reaching but variable effects on local communities. I focus here on interactions between historical actors, and I show how Salasacans in the early twentieth century shaped their ritual practices and attempted to control some aspects of their ongoing evangelization.

There are several studies of the history of the Catholic Church in Ecuador, including a critical analysis by Oswaldo Albornoz (1963) and the studies found in the three-volume *Historia de la iglesia Católica en el Ecuador* (Lara 2001), but little has been written about church-indigenous relations in Ecuador in specific cultural contexts, especially from the point of view of indigenous actors in the early twentieth century (Hamerly 2000; but see Lyons 2006). My goal here is to understand how the general policies of Catholic indoctrination affected the development of ritual life in the specific cultural context of Salasaca. Salasacans to some extent determined how Catholic evangelization would affect them, even traveling to Quito in 1885 to ask church authorities to return a statue of their patron saint and preventing priests from cutting down a sacred Andean tree. In this chapter and the next, I analyze the religious history of the Salasacans based on documents, letters, and oral testimonies that show the interactions between individual actors, including Catholic priests, indigenous festival sponsors, governors, and chapel caretakers. After independence, church officials replaced the old colonial caciques (the traditional indigenous authorities) with indigenous governors and alcaldes. These actors both mediated relations between the Salasacans and the outside authorities (Carrasco A. 1982) and maintained a sense of collective memory and identity within their community. Salasacans shaped the fiesta-cargo system of sponsorship of Catholic feast days into a ritual form for sustaining indigenous memory. The analysis presented here lays the foundation for understanding the subsequent chapters that focus on modernday rituals.

I have not found colonial church documents that refer specifically to Salasaca, but I will briefly describe evangelization in the Audiencia de Quito based on the *Itinerario para párrocos de indios*, a guide written by Archbishop Alonso de la Peña Montenegro in 1668. The New World posed new dilemmas for priests working in indigenous parishes. The vicars of the Ibarra, Cuenca, and Guayaquil dioceses asked the archbishop of Quito to write a standard guide for priests serving indigenous populations, in order to resolve the many questions posed by their new situation. In response to these requests, Archbishop de la Peña wrote the *Itinerario*. This guide provides information on both indigenous ritual practices in the early colonial period and church policy toward dealing with "idolatry." De la Peña condemned the oppression of indigenous people and emphasized the duty of the clergy to protect parishioners from abuse and exploitation, but he also advised certain punishments for idolatry. In the guide de la Peña discussed specific aspects of Andean religious practices, such as the use of a guinea pig in curing rituals and the veneration of sacred hills. Salasacans continue to use both of these native Andean spiritual practices, and there are several personal testimonies about the results of mountain offerings and guinea pig diagnosis (presented in chaps. 7 and 8). De la Peña mentioned the worship of sacred places several times, and noted that even those who had converted to Christianity continued the practice of leaving mountain offerings. Idolatry ranks second among the vices and sins he described (after sodomy and bestiality): "the Indians, even after being converted, have their places of worship, shrines [*guacas*] and idols in the refuge and caves of the mountains to worship and vener-ate them more freely, without suspicion of the priests, whom they fear" (Peña Montenegro 1995 [1668]:337). According to de la Peña, even 135 years after Catholic evangelization the native Andean practices remained strong. Again, de la Peña mentioned mountain worship: "they have tall mountains in their view, large stones, snow-covered mountains, and they rejoice in the splendor of the sun, the moon, and the stars" (463).

Throughout the colonial period, and continuing after independence, the Catholic faith and rituals were taught to indigenous people throughout Ecuador. Efforts to extirpate idolatries transformed but did not eradicate native beliefs and practices, and priests tolerated some native Andean practices. The history of Catholicism in indigenous communities led to the creation of new rituals, ceremonial roles, performances, and prayers. Like many indigenous peoples throughout Latin America, Salasacans incorporated Catholic symbols into their spiritual lives. One specific form this incorporation took was to honor a sacred Andean tree as the source of a Catholic saint.

After Ecuador's independence from Spain and separation from Gran Colombia in 1830, there were slow changes in state-indigenous relations. Native chiefs and subchiefs were slowly replaced with indigenous governors and watchmen called *alcaldes*. Since Salasaca was a rural annex of the parish of Pelileo, priests were not always present in the community but would ride there on horseback once a week to give Catholic spiritual lessons (*la doctrina*). Unfortunately, I have not found any church records on Salasaca during 1861–1875, a period of increased evangelization efforts under the Catholic authoritarian rule of García Moreno (Lane 2003:94; Williams 2005). The earliest document I found is a priest's report from 1885, and it is revealing of the nature of religious practices at the turn of the twentieth century. The 1885 letter tells of an incident involving the repair of the statue of San Buenaventura, housed in the chapel of "Old Salasaca" (the hamlet of Chilcapamba). This relates to a second incident regarding the adoration of a sacred tree, which I suggest was the Andean quishuar (kishwar) tree, in 1907. The letters indicate that some Salasacans believed their sacred tree would give birth to their Catholic patron saint, revealing one means by which people incorporated Catholic icons into Andean cosmological systems.

In their writings, the priests express the view that indigenous people were oppressed by their own superstitions, often referring to "these poor Indians" and their mistaken beliefs. The discourse reveals a combination of pity, paternalistic protectionism, and scorn for indigenous culture. The priests clearly recognize the oppression of indigenous people at the time, and in 1907 Father Carlos María de la Torre, who later became archbishop of Quito, blatantly criticized the church for its treatment of indigenous peoples. I begin with the 1885 report by Father Vicente Melo regarding the statue of San Buenaventura:

Pelileo April 4, 1885.
To the Illustrious Vicar General of the Archdiocese:

In your letter you urge me to inform you about what happened with the statue of San Buenaventura of the chapel of "Salasaca": I do so in the following terms. [It has been] Now three years [since] a part of the said statue was burned. I sent it to be retouched and for this motive a great ruckus occurred among them: some said that I had sold it, others that I had changed it, and they came several times in a tumult to insult me; finally, they were convinced that it was the same statue. Now again, among themselves, I don't know what they have done with the statue; they went to Quito, they brought back a note from Your Excellency, and they turned against me once again, and they showed complete disrespect toward me, so that I had to throw them out of the Parochial House. I didn't want to take part in this matter because I wish such a statue didn't exist; in order to see if in this way one could take out some part of the fanaticism and superstition that exist in this class of people. Because they are so convinced that their Saint was alive, that when they wanted rain they bathed it and when they wanted sun they covered it in sand. They have really done this, and other such things.

Fulfilling the mandate of Your Excellency, I have given my orders to investigate this matter, and I found out that an individual from [the town of] Totoras has it and that the indigenes have taken him to this place.

May God Keep Your Excellency
Vicente Melo. (Melo a Vicario General 1885)

Not willing to accept passively the "changed" statue from the local priest, Father Melo, the Salasacans went over his head and took their case up the Catholic hierarchy:

Your Excellency:

Silverio Masaquiza, Bernardo Jeres, Augustín Pilla, and Félix Jiménes, indigenous people of the Vice Parish of Salasaca in the Pelileo
Canton, to Your Excellency, we present [the following]: that when
we presented to the Venerable priest of Pelileo the provision that
Your Excellency issued on the claim that we made about our Santo
Buenaventura he became very irritated, even getting to the extreme
that at the end of my speaking he beat me ten times with a reed [*diez
bejucasos*], and his houseboy Manuel María gave me three more.
Therefore we inform you of this incident, with the objective that you
take measures so that he returns the saint to us, by means of your
authority. . . .
José Pilla and Vicente Masaquisa, [priostero?] of the church of
Salasaca,
We beseech Your Excellency to decide on this matter what he finds
appropriate. At the request of all interested parties. . . .

(Masaquiza, Jeres, Pilla, and Jiménes al Imo. Señor 1885)

The final signature on the letter, most likely that of a paid scribe, is
illegible. I am not sure which letter was written first, because the letter
from the Salasacans is not dated but is stamped for the years 1884–1885. It
is significant that Father Melo writes of the indigenous delegation going to
Quito, because it shows the determination of the ancestors of modernday
Salasacans to go over the head of the local church authority and appeal to
the higher authorities in the nation's capital to have their statue returned.
Despite the traditionalism and isolation for which Salasacans were known
in the early twentieth century (see Cassagrande 1981), Salasacans actively
sought to control their religious experiences and the nature of their relationship with the institutional church and its representatives.

Father Melo's complaint that the Salasacans would cover the statue
with sand when they wanted sun and with water when they wanted rain is
supported by oral testimony. Older Salasacans recall that the statue could
bring rain, and some say that when it rained too much, the people themselves sent the statue away. But at the time of this letter, some believed that
the priest had stolen their statue. During my fieldwork in the 1990s, when

Salasacans discussed fiestas in honor of San Buenaventura, they always told me that the statue they had was not the original statue.

This dispute, which took place between indigenous people and the priest in 1885, was referred to again in 1907 during a conflict over another object of indigenous veneration: a sacred tree. The first priest to report the practice of leaving offerings to the tree was Luis Octavio Barreno, in a letter dated January 8, 1907 (Barreno a González Suárez 1907):

> To His Excellency Doctor D. Federico González S.,
>   Most Dignified Archbishop of Quito.
> Your Holy Excellency:
>
> With humble greetings to Your Grace: those on whose behalf I write, the Salasacas, request from Your Grace the gift of a statue, of the height of one *vara*, of the most holy Virgin, as the whites have told them that Your Grace has lent various objects of worship to the parish of Rosario, these poor ones come to you to obtain the said image, as in their chapel they have nothing. I take this opportunity to ask of Your Excellency some two crucifixes for the holy mass and two altar stones.
>
> Additionally, I bring to your Grace's knowledge that these poor Indians are worshipping a tree, as they have the idea that a crucifix will be born from the said tree and those who go are the owners of the said tree. So I await your orders about this matter and I hope your Grace concedes what they want, and what I ask [the two crucifixes and two altar stones]. Kissing your ring humbly, Your humble son in Our Lord,
>
> Luis Octavio Barreno.

A second priest, Father Carlos María de la Torre, wrote a detailed report to the archbishop that reveals the conflict between the Andean practice of venerating the tree and the church's attempts to replace indigenous sacred shrines with Catholic imagery (de la Torre 1907a). Whereas Father Barreno referred to the belief that a crucifix would emerge from the tree, Father de la Torre reported the belief that the statue of San Buenaventura would be born from the trunk, the *same* statue that Salasacans said had been stolen from them in 1885.

Father de la Torre's letter provides some insight into the difficulties priests faced during their ongoing evangelization efforts. In both his written report and the oral memories of elderly Salasacans we get an image of the priest riding on horseback to give spiritual lessons in the indigenous outlying rural areas that surround the central parish. In his letter to the archbishop of Quito, dated January 23, 1907, Father de la Torre first described his work in the areas surrounding the mother parish of Pelileo. After discussing the lack of morality in Pelileo, which he blamed on the influence of liberalism ("because of Pelileo's proximity to Ambato"), Father de la Torre complained that people were asking him to baptize their babies at 6 or 7 p.m., so that "decent people" would not have their babies baptized alongside people from the countryside. He explained to these urban elites that God does not recognize social distinctions and that the church welcomes all equally to its breast. "Before God and his church, there are no distinctions in the administration of sacraments, there are no social distinctions, there are only souls." De la Torre also mentioned a lack of instruction in church teachings. But the spiritual necessities of the parishioners in the annexes had caused him temporarily to leave this pastoral work. He would ride on horseback for an hour to go to the new parish of Rosario on festival days to say mass, and then three-quarters of an hour (from the center of Pelileo) to the mountain Teligote. His letter then turns to the Salasacans:

> Among the Salasacas, who constitute one of the parts of the new parish of Rosario, a superstition has been introduced that until now has been impossible to extirpate. There exists a small tree, or rather a bush, that with its two roots penetrates the soil. Well, the feverish fantasy of the indigenes, enlivened by the blow of the demon, has found legs in those roots, and in the natural outgrowth of the trunk, the womb of a person, and in this way they have propagated the original idea that the tree is pregnant with San Buenaventura (specifically with a statue that they possessed in past times and that, according to what they say, was stolen by Father Melo). One of them has had a dream in which he has seen that the tree is going to give birth to the statue, and all the indigenes are awaiting from one moment to the next such a marvelous birth. Two days before Sr. Barreno was to arrive I went personally to the place where the tree is and I didn't find anything,

absolutely nothing extraordinary. The worst part is (and this demonstrates the lamentable ignorance of these peoples) that many whites
have allowed the sedition of the Indians and have cooperated with
the superstition by offering [candles?] to the formless trunk of the
tree. In fulfillment of my duties I exhorted from the pulpit to abstain
from such manifestations and with the authority of pastor I prohibited
pilgrimages to the tree. It seems I have been obeyed, but not on the part
of the Salasacans themselves, to whom I could not speak personally
because of my ignorance of Quichua. Nevertheless I proposed that
they cut down the tree and from the same wood I would give them a
S. Buenaventura or other image. It seemed they were convinced, but
when the moment arrived to fulfill the pact they denied it. Afterwards,
Father Barreno proposed the formation of an image in the tree itself,
without cutting it down, and they did not agree to this proposal. These
poor indigenes have not participated in civilization but rather in vices
that degrade them: they are the most frequent and generous consumers
of alcoholic beverages.

De la Torre goes on to recommend that the church

send [to Salasaca], for at least one year, a priest according to the heart
of God, who sees only the divine glory and the good of the souls, that
he live with them, that he loves them, yes, above all that he loves them
a lot, and therefore that he doesn't treat them as is often done with the
poor Indians, in verga ferrea ["with the iron scourge"], with whippings
and lashings, insults and harshness, but rather with softness, sweetness,
and compassion . . . in a large part the despicable state in which the
indigenous race finds itself is due to this cruel and inhumane treatment. The Indian has lost the idea of human dignity: will he recover
it someday? When a minister of God treats him as one would treat a
beast? (de la Torre 1907a)

This letter is significant for several features. The discourse of the letter
matches the style of nineteenth-century representations of poor, ignorant
Indians in a miserable state (Guerrero 1997). Then the priest's own sense
of social equality becomes clear, as he argues against local blanco-mestizos
who do not wish to have their children baptized with peasants. This was

most likely a racial rather than a geographic distinction; it is an example of what Jean Rahier (1998) calls "the racial/spatial order" in Ecuador. That is, it is implied that the people of the countryside are "more Indian" than their urban-dwelling neighbors (see Radcliffe and Westwood 1996).

The letter reveals the frustration of an individual priest over the harsh mistreatment of indigenous peoples in highland Ecuador. De la Torre requests that a priest come to serve the people, one who "above all . . . loves them a lot." He seems to be aware that a Salasacan had a dream revelation about the emergence of the statue of San Buenaventura from the tree. We don't know how he came across this information, but it shows his understanding of the significance of dreams in Salasaca. Although both Father Barreno and Father de la Torre were guided by the attitude that the Indians were oppressed by their own superstition, they were willing to work with indigenous beliefs, creatively suggesting a means of incorporating "superstition," in the form of wood from a sacred tree, into the Catholic pantheon of saints. Still, even this accommodation was rejected by the Salasacans, who saw no conflict between their Catholic saint and the adoration of the sacred tree. I found no letters after this date to indicate what happened; the next letter that refers to Salasaca is dated January 29, 1907, and confirms that the Salasacans received a statue of the Virgin which was "very well received by all the natives such that all, with drums [*tambores*] and dancers have taken it to their chapel" (de la Torre 1907b).

The tree to which the priest refers is most likely the quishuar tree, sacred to Andeans since pre-Columbian times. De la Torre's description of a "small tree, or rather a bush" fits the quishuar, which is described as a small tree or shrub. His statement that people believed the tree was going to "give birth" to the saint can be compared to a Salasacan narrative that describes a saint slowly emerging from the trunk of a quishuar tree. Although the Salasacan narrative describes a "virgin" emerging from the tree, rather than San Buenaventura, I believe both narratives refer to the same incident, but there were different interpretations of what would emerge from the sacred tree (a crucifix, a virgin, or San Buenaventura). The belief that an Andean sacred tree would give birth to a Catholic icon is one local manifestation of religious transculturation, the way by which "subordinated or marginal groups select and invent from materials transmitted to them by a dominant or metropolitan culture" (Pratt 1992:6).

The quishuar (*Buddelei longifolia*) is a short Andean tree to which people from Ecuador, Peru, and Bolivia attribute supernatural powers. Colonial documents make references to the ritual use of quishuar trees. The Incas used quishuar wood to make religious objects (MacCormack 1991:170). In the seventeenth century Father Bernabé Cobo wrote of a place called Quishuarpugio, a spring from which Inca soldiers drank after a battle (Cobo and Hamilton 1990:62). *The Huarochirí Manuscript* contains the story of a woman named Chuqi Suso who was worshipped by the people: "In worshipping her, they built a quishuar enclosure and stayed inside it for five days without ever letting people walk outside" (Salomon and Urioste 1991:64). The early colonial references to the ceremonial use of quishuar trees are evidence that the Salasacan stories about the quishuar reflect the continuation of a pre-Columbian Andean tradition. In the 1950s, the Costales reported stories about offerings to a quishuar tree in Salasaca, until one day it disappeared (Peñaherrera de Costales and Costales Samaniego 1959: 86). Salasacans told me about two places where sacred quishuar trees existed. One was in the hamlet of Ramos Loma, and some report that the name of the hamlet used to be Ramos Loma Quishuar. According to a male elder from Ramos Loma, there was a courtyard of quishuar trees in the shape of a cross, and the central tree was sacred. One elder from this hamlet stated, "The baby Jesus was born in the quishuar tree. They are not to be cut down and thrown away. Only after cutting down the quishuar trees did we have frost here." He also affirmed that Salasacans had their own quishuar, like the Lord of Cuicuno, a sacred quishuar in Cotopaxi Province (Moya 1981:78). The trees in Ramos Loma, Salasaca, were uprooted and destroyed, and the region subsequently suffered from two years of frost. Today, only the central tree stands, and I am not aware of any special offerings to it.

The other quishuar tree was located near a spring above the sacred crossroads of Cruz Pamba on the route up Catitagua, which is one of a series of mountains containing shrines near the border of Salasaca (see fig. 1.3 and Wogan 2004:121–22). According to some, the indigenous people didn't want mestizos to take their water, so they covered the spring with rocks, and it dried up. Others say that a menstruating *soltera* (unmarried young woman) bathed in the spring and caused it to dry up. Marta, a female Salasacan elder, described the spring and the sacred quishuar (which she called *quishuri*) of Catitagua, as her own grandmother had described it to her.

Marta's grandmother was a child when she discovered the "virgin" (which she uses interchangeably with "saint" in her narrative) in the quishuar tree. She had discovered it while pasturing sheep, but she didn't tell anyone. One day, on the Day of the Dead (*finados*), the grandmother's mother went to mass and visited the old cemetery in Pelileo to "feed" her deceased family members. The mother left the children at home alone. The children said, "Let's play Caporales!" They dressed up as the characters from the Caporales fiesta and went to the hill to play. That's when Marta's grandmother told the other children about the virgin in the quishuar tree: "Up there is a virgin. It was up there in Cruz Pamba, indeed in the quishuri tree there was a saint, like this [indicating that it was just the face that appeared], I saw it. It was in the quishuri tree." (*Jahuapiga shug virgin tiagushca . . . Jahuapimi tiashca, Cruz Pambapi, quishuri yurapimi santo tiacurga cashnahualla, cashnahualla ricurgani . . . Quishuri yurapi tiashcami.*)

She showed them the saint and, dressed as festival characters, the children circled around the tree. But the children still didn't tell their mother or anyone else about the saint. After playing, they returned home. The next day, their mother was preparing to go to the Day of the Dead mass in Pelileo when a neighbor who had seen the children playing came riding up on a horse, carrying a liter of sugarcane alcohol. He called out to the children as if they were sponsors of the fiesta of Caporales: "Hey Tayta Caporal! Mama Fundadora!" he yelled. Their mother asked, "What is he talking about?" At first the children pretended not to know, but their mother beat them until they cried and told her the truth. Marta recounted in detail the dialogue between her grandmother and great-grandmother:

> "There is a saint up there. A dear little saint has been up there. I saw it! Yesterday we were playing Caporales."
>
> "Where is it? Where is this saint? And you'd better not be lying."
>
> "I'm not lying."
>
> "Then let's go and you show me. You lead the way so that you can show me."

So the child fastened her little shawl, and she led her mother to the tree. "Here it is" she said, and she showed the saint to her mother. Marta's grandmother told her: "That's when I spoke about [the apparition]. It was appearing in the trunk of the tree, in the trunk of the tree it was stuck like this, just the face. It appeared in the trunk. In the trunk of the big quishuri, it was stuck there. Mama said, 'Indeed it's true.'"

Then all the people gathered there, and they held a fiesta. Marta's grandmother, although she was a child, was the founder of that fiesta. But so many people would go to the tree and the spring, including bad people and menstruating women, that the spring and the tree disappeared. As Marta said, "The tree was just lost, the quishuri also dried up; it dried up, the quishuri also. When it dried up the saint was lost." (*Yurallatapi chingun, quishurish chaquin, chaquinmi quishurish. Chaquiriquiga chingun santo.*)

Marta added that the people had begun to construct a wall around the tree, and part of the crumbling wall could still be seen on the hill above Cruz Pamba. The virgin, she said, had been becoming clearer each day (emerging from the tree) but started to disappear when too many people went there.

We can compare the two reports about venerating a sacred tree: the 1907 priest's written report in Spanish and the oral story told by Marta in Quichua. The narratives reflect the process of religious transculturation from two different positions in the contact zone, described by Mary Louise Pratt (1992:6) as "the space in which peoples geographically and historically separated come into contact with each other and establish ongoing relations, usually involving conditions of coercion, radical inequality, and intractable conflict." Although indigenous people had been in contact with the Eurocentric Catholic Church since the early colonial period, the process of religious transculturation was still ongoing in 1907. Pratt's use of the term *contact* emphasizes the interactions of individuals within the space of a cultural encounter.

Marta's oral narrative provides a sense of the indigenous perspective on the sacred tree. Most likely the discourse about what exactly was emerging from the tree varied among Salasacans. Marta's story makes no mention of a pregnancy, roots as legs, or San Buenaventura. Rather, she describes a miraculous tree in whose trunk an image began to appear. Her Quichua narrative is what survives of a memory orally transmitted from a woman to her granddaughter, a memory sustained by female genealogical links in the founding family dedicated to this saint. The story focuses on details such as the geographical location of the tree (sacred space), the context in which the saint was discovered, and the temporal context (sacred time). Marta's story reflects several characteristics of Quechua storytelling described by Rosaleen Howard:

> the single most powerful factor in the operation of memory in the oral tradition is the association that narrators make between the local landscape (context of their own lives) and the events of the stories they tell. . . . Analysis of these texts suggests a cognitive relationship between land and language that I believe holds the key to the way the oral tradition is continually regenerated in human memory, and a study of which can reinforce our appreciation of the significance of the landscape in all aspects of Andean thought. (Howard 2002:30)

Memory and landscape are mutually sustained in Andean ways of knowing. Memory is engraved in topographic spaces, and in Quichua oral recollections events are organized in relationship to the festival cycle; that is, around sacred time. In her narrative, Marta states that the event occurred on the day of finados, when the mother had gone to mass and to the old cemetery in Pelileo to visit the graves of her ancestors and exchange bread with other Salasacans. That's when the children saw the saint and circled the tree. The context was the children's pretending to perform a fiesta, which was a common play activity among children when their parents would send them to the hills to pasture sheep.

Marta's narrative contains several characteristics of Quechua speech, including the use of parallelism ("the quishuri also dried up; it dried up, the quishuri also") and "embedded discourse," the insertion of the words and even thoughts of other people into the discourse (Mannheim and Van Vleet 1998). Marta inserts bits of conversations between the protagonists in the narrative, and uses the words *nishca* (she had said) and *nishcami* (indeed she had said) to affirm that she is repeating what her grandmother told her. She includes important cultural details about the context of the discovery: how her grandmother and the other children were pasturing sheep and playing fiesta; the secrecy in which the children guarded their discovery; and how it was converted from a children's play fiesta to a real fiesta, with Marta's grandmother as the *fundadora*, when adults became aware of the saint. The fundadora is the person responsible for ensuring that the fiesta is continued in the saint's honor, and this responsibility is passed down through genealogical links (Lyons 2006).

The letter from Father Carlos María de la Torre, on the other hand, relates details about some Salasacan beliefs. He recounts that one of the Salasacans had a dream that the tree was going to give birth to a statue of San Buenaventura. Perhaps some Salasacans did believe that the very same statue that was "stolen" in 1885 would come back through this sacred Andean tree. De la Torre's letter is interesting because it reveals how the priests tried to negotiate with the Salasacans as part of the process of transculturation that takes place in the contact zones where different cultures interact. On one side the indigenous people were determined to continue their own religious practices and leave offerings to a tree that has been sacred in the Andes since pre-Columbian times. On the other side was a minister of the Catholic Church, charged with evangelizing people and carrying out ecclesiastical orders from Quito. He attempted to compromise with the Salasacans by proposing that a saint's image be carved from the tree, but this was rejected by the Salasacans. In rural parishes, the priests were the agents who had to implement the policies decided in the nation's capital. The letter reveals those conflicts and the negotiations that took place between the people practicing a local form of religion, the institution of the Catholic Church, and the priest as a mediator. In his report de la Torre uses the incident to criticize the treatment of indigenous people in Ecuador. His report to the archbishop moves from a description of Salasacan "superstitions" to a protest against the oppression of indigenous people.

The story of the quishuar tree shows the complexity of the process of evangelization and the back-and-forth negotiations that took place between the institutional church and the actors involved. It is an example of the localization of the dominant religion within Salasacan sacred space: the quishuar was located on the hill Catitagua between the crossroads of Cruz Pamba and the mountain Quinchi Urcu. As Pratt (1992:6) writes, "While subjugated peoples cannot readily control what emanates from the dominant culture, they do determine to varying extents what they absorb into their own, and what they use it for." One colonial product that indigenous people used to their own purposes was the fiesta sponsorship system. The social roles associated with sponsorship of Catholic feast days became one of the most prominent representations of indigenous tradition. In the next chapter I show how indigenous actors engaged church authorities over positions of festival sponsorship.

CHAPTER 3

Textual Strategies and Ritual Control in Early Twentieth-Century Salasaca

THE FIESTA SPONSORSHIP SYSTEM is a quintessential example of a colonial imposition that was transformed into a symbol of indigenous cultural identity. By the early twentieth century, indigenous men were vying for the priests' favor in order to be named as festival sponsors. I focus here on specific interactions between indigenous Salasacans and the Catholic clergy from 1908 to 1914. Letters and telegrams, which are among the few bits of preserved correspondence between indigenous people and higher church authorities in Quito, indicate the importance of the fiesta-cargo system to early twentieth-century Salasacans. In the final part of this chapter I analyze oral histories of catechism in the memories of two elderly Salasacan women.

Catholic authorities in colonial Latin America implemented a system of indigenous sponsorship of saints' day celebrations in order to increase indigenous engagement with the church. By selecting fundadores (individuals to be responsible for fiesta celebrations for particular saints or feast days), as well as other indigenous officials such as alcaldes and *priostes*, the church authorities could use the fiesta system to bring indigenous people into the faith. In indigenous communities in Mexico, Central America, and the Andes, the institution of fiesta sponsorship is known as the fiesta-cargo system. Traditionally, a man agrees to take on the burden (*cargo*) of serving the community as an authority and a sponsor of Catholic feast-day celebrations.[1] The occupation of a specific cargo for the year is marked by the sponsor's possession of a staff of authority, called a *vara*. Although the sponsor often goes into debt as a result of taking on the position, he gains respect and prestige in the community. The Salasacans incorporated the fiesta-cargo system into their culture, where it became a pervasive aspect of kinship relations, cosmology, sacred geography, and collective life. For example, fiesta sponsors call on family members and ritual kin, such as matrimonial godchildren, to help with the labor and expenses of sponsoring a fiesta. Evidence of the importance of the fiesta-cargo system to indigenous people can be found in parish archives from the early twentieth century. These archives contain letters to church authorities regarding disputes within the community over festival sponsorship, and the correspondence between indigenous people and clerics shows how individuals interacted with the institutional church in making decisions about the festive-ritual life of their community.

Salasacans engaged church authorities in their attempts to control the appointment of ritual cargo holders, and they employed textual strategies to persuade clerics of their arguments. Priests preferred to appoint literate indigenous men to serve as governors of Salasaca, and these men wrote letters directly to the archbishop to address concerns about priests and sponsorship positions. For example, in 1908 Manuel Caizabanda, the governor of Salasaca, wrote to the archbishop to complain that the local priest was charging a fee for masses. He also sent a list of names of men who wanted to serve as alcaldes (Caizabanda a Arzobispo 1908). Governors were not the only individuals who communicated their concerns to the authorities in Quito: common, illiterate Salasacans hired scribes to manipulate religious discourse in their letters to the vicar-general and the archbishop. This is one strategy through which Salasacans attempted to control the ritual life of their community. I will analyze several letters written in the early 1900s. The first letter involves two men: Agustín Masaquiza and Rudecindo Masaquiza, who were competing for the position of "alcalde mayor de las doctrinas" (the lead alcalde). On New Year's Day each year, the priest names the new alcaldes and the alcalde mayor for that year, but the candidates for the position start competing a year or more ahead of time. In 1908 Agustín and Rudecindo were competing for the position, and Salasacans were supporting either one candidate or the other. Upon hearing this, the archbishop requested that the priest send both candidates to him so that he could meet them personally and decide which one would serve (Sánchez 1908). On October 17, 1908, the acting alcalde mayor of Salasaca sent a telegram to the archbishop of Quito stating, "Agustín Masaquisa has been named alcalde mayor since the New Year, and it is not true that he has taken the alcaldeship [alcaldazgo] from Rudecindo Masaquiza" (Cuato al Arzobispo 1908). But the local priest denied that Agustín Masaquiza had been named and wrote a letter to the subsecretary of the curia, asking him to communicate to the archbishop:

that on the sixteenth I notified Agustín Matsaquitsa and Rudecindo Matsaquitsa [*sic*] so that they would present themselves before the Holy Curia. . . .So that the maliciousness of these Indians does not distort the truth, I tell you that the indigenous men of whom you speak, and to whom I refer, are the father of Rudecindo, Manuel Jiménez, and Rudecindo himself. All these have lied to the authorities: it is false that Agustín Masaquiza has been named alcalde mayor, it is also false that Rudecindo Masaquiza has displaced him of his position. The alcalde mayor of Salasaca in this year is Nicolás Jiménez. Agustín and Rudecindo *ask* that they be named one of the alcaldes of the year 1909 on the first of January of this year. (Carrillo a Subsecretario 1908)

Since the priest was in the process of transporting stone blocks to the church, he decided that whichever of Agustín or Rudecindo transported the stones for him would be named alcalde mayor for 1909, and the other for the year 1910, adding "perhaps the Monsignor will reprimand me for this, but . . . it is a very old custom that the candidate for the alcaldeship" serve the parish priest for a year (Carrillo a Subsecretario 1908).

This letter refers to an old custom for selecting festival sponsors, and the following year Rudecindo Masaquiza wrote to the archbishop, giving details of all of his sacrifices and service to the church, including paying for building materials from a local quarry and renting mules to have the materials transported to the church. For this reason, he argued, he deserved to be named alcalde mayor (Masaquiza a Arzobispo 1908).

In a letter to the subsecretary of the Bishopric of Quito, Father Carrillo praised the candidate for governor of Salasaca, Matías Chango, as "the best Indian; he knows how to read and write, and will make up for the incompetence" of the two candidates for alcalde mayor. Father Carrillo said he would prefer that a third candidate, Pedro Anancolla, be the alcalde mayor, rather than either of the two "troublemakers" who were contending for the position. Although Pedro Anancolla had not sought the position, the priest believed he was best qualified for it (Carrillo a Subsecretario 1908). I did not find any document recording who won the position, but the telegrams and letters sent by both indigenous men and the clergymen show that the competition to be named alcalde mayor was intense.

Priests and indigenous men had different ideas about the significance of being alcalde mayor. For the indigenous men, official positions entailed social prestige and some limited authority within the community, but the priests were concerned with finding someone who was literate and met their standards for morality. In 1910, another priest from Pelileo wrote to the vicar about how difficult it was to get indigenous people in the rural annexes to come together for religious instruction. But among the Salasacans, he said,

> Some of them come. As I have seen that these have governors, alcaldes, *alguaciles*, and *fiscales*, I want to ask your excellency, can I keep naming the [officeholders]? I have gotten the governor of the Indians of Salasaca (an Indian who is very skillful in the doctrina and very smart) to confess five times a year, achieving that his exterior conduct is set. . . . I have two of his sons in school, to see if later I can place them as *maestros* in this district; the Indians will not accept a white maestro — can I name alcaldes? (Ferán a Vicario 1910)

The priest requested the authority to name governors, maestros, and alcaldes because these men served to unite the other indigenous people, enforce their attendance at religious lessons, mediate Catholic teachings, and ensure participation in observances of Catholic feast days. The interactions and negotiations that were taking place between indigenous individuals, between priests and indigenous people, and between priests and their superiors show how the function of governors, festival sponsors, and maestros as mediators between indigenous people and church officials was still developing in the early twentieth century.

A later dispute arose over the inheritance of the office of *pendonero*, which was at one time one of the most prestigious sponsorship positions. In a 1913 letter to the archbishop, the indigenous petitioners employ the persuasive strategy of referring to themselves as poor and ignorant. At the same time they reveal their knowledge of the "laws of the Spanish Regime" in that they use descent from their grandfather as a justification to wrestle the position from another male relative.[2] They urged the archbishop to expedite the resolution in time for the upcoming festivities of Corpus Christi. I present excerpts of that letter here to show the textual strategies employed by the scribe on behalf of the petitioners:

> José and Gerónimo Jerez and Ignacio Anancolla, to your Excellency, we come to you to make the following statement: that in our Canton

of Pelileo, Province of Tungurahua, with the proper permission, we state: that since time immemorial, it has happened that because of his virtue and honor our antecessor Manuel Masaquiza had received through superior command the title of Pindonero [*sic*] and fundador of this fiesta, to preserve for life and by authority of the Ecclesiastical Authority, which ordered that this title be passed on to his descendants, as it was established in the laws of the Spanish Regime.

Now, without having knowledge of the very many sacrifices made by our antecessor Manuel Masaquisa to get this title, Mariano Masaquiza the younger has appropriated this title on the basis of having been the brother of our antecessor, but without authorization of any ecclesiastical, much less civil, authority.

As the representatives we are the grandsons of the aforementioned Manuel Masaquisa, and by direct line we have the right of receiving this distinction given by the proper authorities and, because our antecessor was conferred the title of pindonero more than sixty years ago when this distinction was established; we have the right, as his legitimate successors, to request that Your Excellency, order the Señor Vicario Foraneo of the Region of Pelileo [to grant] the material possession to those us, the undersigned, and to revoke Mariano Masaquiza's use of the title of pindonero, considering that we, the undersigned, are the sole inheritors of the same father.

Your Excellency, you know that custom among indigenous people becomes the law [*la costumbre entre indígenas hace ley*]. Please take into account that people who are prone to profit from any source take advantage of us because they see us as ignorant, but happily we have a pastor like Your Excellency, who watches over his poor parishioners.

. . . We do believe Your Excellency's resolution should be favorable: it shall be ordered that the Priest of our aforementioned region should get the banner [*pindón*] back in the same condition in which it was given and that he deliver it to us in good condition, so [that we may] venerate and continue to worship as our Religion proscribes.

On behalf of José and Gerónimo Jerez and Ignacio Anancolla, who don't know how to write, and as a witness.

Román Castillo, Vicaría General de la Arquidiócis. (Jerez and Anancolla al Arzobispo 1913)

The writer of the letter appeals to the archbishop's sense of justice in making his case, arguing that because the archbishop is a good man he will find in favor of the grandsons' appeal. It is a common strategy in verbal art to appeal to tradition and precedent as persuasive tools. The scribe refers to both the "laws of the Spanish Regime" and "custom among indigenous people" in the letter. In the closing paragraph, the writer makes an appeal to religion as well. Speaking for the indigenous petitioners, he writes that the Salasacan clients want the banner so that they can "venerate and worship as our Religion orders," thereby using the desire of indigenous people to be good Catholics as a strategy to persuade the archbishop to find in their favor. Although the grandsons of Manuel Masaquiza were the ones demanding rights of inheritance to the position, the letter was actually written for them by Ramón Castillo of the office of the vicar. Note that the letters and telegrams follow a discourse that was common in late nineteenth-century documents on indigenous Ecuadorians. Indigenous peoples were variously labeled as miserable, unfortunate, and ignorant in order to meet certain political ends (Guerrero 1997). Since telegrams and letters were typically written on behalf of the Salasacans by a third person, we do not know whether indigenous peoples referred to themselves this way or if the writer imposed this interpretation on the indigenous state-ments. Nor do we know whether the writer manipulated the statements to suit his own goals. Even if the individuals who paid for the letters and telegrams were accurately represented, we must keep in mind that they were acting as individuals, perhaps without disclosing their actions to other Salasacans.

Andrés Guerrero suggests that it was the scribes, who knew how to play the political game, that introduced such textual strategies:

> The function of the scribe who produces the document is not entirely derived from his control over the writing. It is also not reduced to the problem of translating, from the tongue (oral Quechua) of the populations that the governor of natives represents, to the language [written Spanish] of the republic and its citizens. The unknown inter-mediary carries out at least two additional functions. On the one hand, he becomes a ventriloquist because he makes a voiceless indigenous authority speak in the public-state sphere. He presents the problem in the state's code; he assembles a legitimate and legal discourse. On

the other hand, as he writes the "representation," he is the author of a strategy. (Guerrero 2003:303)

Guerrero focused on letters to civil and state authorities, but the same ventriloquism took place when scribes wrote to ecclesiastical authorities. Despite this textual transculturation, it was indigenous people who were paying for the telegrams and hiring the scribes as intermediaries in order to communicate their desires to the archbishop. As Erin O'Connor (2007:47) shows, although scribes imposed their own language on indigenous petitions, indigenous people understood the politics of the system in which they operated and used the language of the state in their attempts to win disputes. Illiteracy did not stop indigenous people from attempting to exercise some degree of control over their ritual lives, be it through selecting festival sponsors or keeping a particular priest as their pastor, as in the following letter I present. The appropriation of religion and the use of an impoverishing discourse to refer to indigenous people are even more pronounced in it:

January 12, 1914
To the Most Reverend Archbishop of the Archdiocese of Quito.

The residents of the caserío of Salasaca, belonging to the Pelileo Canton, Province of Tungurahua, with the necessary permission, present ourselves before Your Grace, and we explain: That we have knowledge that by your authority you are going to remove the priest Dr. Luis Fernando Bucheli from us and our territory. Although we are ignorant, we know that the said Señor Doctor has a virtuous and charitable heart, in particular with the unfortunate ones [*infelices*]; we have the right, in the name of all our caserío, to demand [the continued appointment of] the worthy Señor Doctor Bucheli, who in the time in which he has guided us, has instilled in us in few days the precept of loving God and the people; and particularly he wishes the well-being of all, and he wishes to establish the Catholic faith in everyone in general and particularly in the indigenous people.

It seems to us that Señor Doctor Bucheli has arrived at the heart of our community to serve as Pastor of the souls of we who search for salvation. It seems to us, we believe, that not only we, the *unfortunate ones* of Salasaca, claim the worthiness of Señor Doctor Bucheli, but also everyone in general, based on the virtues and charity that he displays, to this Worthy Prelate.

We do not doubt, Your Holy Excellency, that in view of this humble petition, you will see that we wish to have support in the Religion, one who will *guide us toward the right path*, as he does, one who never departs from the Law given by Our Lord Jesus Christ.

We hope, once again, Your Excellency, that upon receiving our righteous claim, you will order that our Prelate continues to hold, in the Region of Pelileo, the role which he currently holds.

We honor your resolution and will abide by your decision.

Salasaca, January 12, 1914—At the request of the vecinos of Salasaca who don't know how to sign their names. [signed] Benjamin Moreno. (Vecinos de Salasaca al Arzobispo 1914; emphasis mine).

In this case, indigenous people sought out the services of a scribe who used the discourse of the church and state in order to influence decisions about which priest would serve them. The strategy employed here is to present the indigenous Salasacans as ignorant and unfortunate, yet dedicated to the Catholic faith and yearning for religious guidance. The metaphor of "choosing the right path" appears in the text of a Quichua prayer (see chap. 5) and indicates that it was part of Catholic evangelizing discourse appropriated by indigenous peoples in their own sacred texts.

In 1914 there was also a dispute over the position of alcalde mayor. The letter regarding this issue, however, is signed by a Salasacan named Raimundo Chango, governor of Salasaca, rather than by a mestizo scribe. The letter is addressed to Archbishop Federico González Suárez.

Ambato, December 18, 1914.
To Archbishop Federico González Suárez
Your Excellency:

My objective being that the annex (Salasaca) [functions] well in the civil and moral [domains], in my capacity as Governor of the said annex, it is my duty to see that the employees of this place be good people and not corrupt and bad. Since at present the one who solicits [the office of alcalde] is prone to vice, as is Agustín Masaquiza, who currently requests [the office of alcalde]. He tricked the Priest of

Pelileo, with his gifts and lies; he wants to replace the current Alcalde, Matías Chango, [on the] first [of January] for the coming year; as Governor and native son of Salasaca I know all the people. So that order proceeds, I beg Your Excellency not to allow that they name Agustín Masaquisa nor confirm the one who currently holds the post. If my words and my good integrity have enough merit for Your Excellency you will name Eduardo Chango as alcalde on the first of the coming year, and if it is not too much, [I ask] that I continue with my same post so that I am responsible for the person I recommend or for any disruption that may come. Hoping you will address my concerns and that you will reply, despite my humble position, and because of the education and greatness of Your Excellency, Your Humble Subject, Raimundo Chango. (Chango al Arzobispo 1914)

The indigenous governor uses flattery to persuade the archbishop and also argues that the local priest was tricked by an indigenous person competing for the position of alcalde mayor. This letter exemplifies the mediating role of these literate, indigenous governors. Priests recommended men for the position of governor based on their ability to read and write, their exemplary character, and their willingness to work with the church on indoctrinating their subordinates. The governor had direct influence on the archbishop's choice of alcalde mayor and clearly favors one man over another. He cleverly points out that he is in a position to make such a recommendation "as governor and son of Salasaca," suggesting that he knows the people well enough to evaluate their qualifications for office. These indigenous governors served as authorities after the abolition of colonial-era caciques (whose main duty was tribute collection), and they were later replaced by the civil *teniente político*. The letters I have presented here show that during the first two decades of the twentieth century, indigenous people incorporated Catholic rituals and teachings through the mediation of church-appointed governors and festival sponsors.

The few reports in church archives from the 1920s and 1930s speak mainly of the need to use Quichua rather than Spanish in indoctrinating the Salasacans, and the difficulty in finding a priest who could perform catechisms in Quichua was an ongoing concern for the church. Although catechism of the Salasacans took place prior to the arrival of the Madres

Lauritas nuns in 1945, the instruction was sporadic and flawed by the priests' lack of knowledge of Quichua. The sponsorship of Catholic feast days continued to flourish in the parish, but only upon the arrival of the nuns was there a permanent presence of Catholic teachers in Salasaca.

Oral Histories of Catechism

The correspondence presented to this point tells the history of catechism in Salasaca based mainly on written reports. It is appropriate to compare this history with the memories of Salasacans based on oral testimonies. I interviewed two women about their memories of the Catholic religious teachings called *la doctrina*. One was Rosa, the mother of Marta, who narrated the story of the miraculous quishuar tree.

Rosa told of her memories of la doctrina:

> When I was a girl I would go to bathe at the spring in the gorge in order to go to the church of Chilcapamba for mass. We would just go, leaving the *pondo* [clay vessel for carrying water] on top of a century plant; sometimes we would steal each other's pondos, other times we would just make the water spill. We would go on like that. Saying, "Mama will scold us again when we get home," we would take the pondo and go back to get water from the spring after coming out of la doctrina. The late Matías Chango, Diomingo Chango of Huambalo, Bitio Caizabanda, Roja Doctor, they would make us pray, "You have to learn to [properly] greet people" they would say, all that. They would make me make the sign of the cross, saying: "Holy Cross, let your will be done, to we who knew nothing [*aucagunamunda*], forgive us [and] "that you are a child of God, in the Holy Spirit, amen." This is what Bitio Caizabanda and Roja Doctor taught us to do. They weren't alcaldes, they were only *rezachij gobernadores* [prayer-maker governors]. They were always advising people. "You must always greet someone when you meet them," they would say. Nowadays [*cunun timpoguna*] upon seeing a person, neither the young men nor the young women greet them; in the past we always exchanged greetings upon an encounter with someone. The elders taught the children to pray in the church in Chilcapamba. They taught them to make the sign of the cross, and to greet. That's how we were when we were children.

Now after getting married I didn't go to bathe [at the spring] or to mass, only occasionally would I go. We got married in Pelileo among ten couples. We had to stay there helping the priest [*curada sirvisha*]. We were there for one month. There they taught us to pray, "that you may live well with your husband" they would say, and they gave us all kinds of advice. I lived there four weeks with my husband, the two of us. In order for us to cook and eat, they gave us barley, peas, potatoes, corn, squash, pumpkin, they gave us all that, saying, "You can cook this and eat it." That's how we lived, and we were married in Pelileo. Now I occasionally go to the mass and the fiestas, too. When my husband was alive we would go together. The nuns used to live in Chilcapamba; after the earthquake they came up to live here [i.e., in the central plaza]; the Mothers Melaña, Luz María, they came first. Now there are new nuns. We used to go to Chilcapamba for mass on Thursdays, and on Sundays the mass was in Pelileo. We would go there. The father would speak Quichua, he would tell us, "Live asking God, don't hit your husband, and live well." He would say "without causing anger," and it was good advice.

Rosa used the word *aucagunamunda* in her narration, which means "from the aucas" but which her grandson translated as "ones who know nothing." The word *auca* has different meanings that derive from historical contexts. A basic meaning is "not baptized." Salasacans will jokingly refer to an unbaptized child as an "auca." Similarly, children who don't eat Salasacan cultivated foods, such as squash, may be teasingly called "auca" by their parents. *Auca* is a pejorative term for the Huaorani people of the Amazonian region. It is interesting, then, that Rosa recalls the line "we who knew nothing [*aucagunamunda*]" as one of the first prayers children were taught when they made the sign of the cross. I believe this relates most closely to the definition of *auca* as one who is not baptized or, by extension, a people who have not yet been converted to Christianity. This prayer was taught by men who seemed to fill the role of early catechists in Salasaca, indigenous men who would learn teachings and prayers from the priest and teach them to young people. Rosa refers to them as "prayer-maker governors," a term I have not heard elsewhere.

Another elderly woman, Manuela, recalled the priest named Father Galves, who served Salasaca in the 1920s:

Father Galves went around on horseback, and in order to feed us he would bring bread, saying to everyone, "Be careful, you might not come [to the doctrina]." First the church was in Chilcapamba, there the alcaldes would talk among themselves; that priest sent them, he made them alcaldes. In the past, some couples would just join together and live, they would gather those people together in order to send them to make them get married. The alcaldes would get them at night to make them get married. Just like that, taking people to the doctrina. That priest ordered it. But my father said that he [Father Galves] wasn't the first priest, there was another priest he said, but he didn't say his name. When I walked around as a *malta mara* [growing adolescent], it was the one called Padre Galves. On the other hand, the nuns also were around; their names were Mother Melaña, Monjorrez, they also were first in Chilcapamba, afterwards they came up, after the earthquake they came up. Today, there is this church here too, in our so-called center. Just like that, in the past, in the mornings we would go to bathe in the spring at four in the morning. Afterwards, we would go to hear the mass in Pelileo. By foot we would go; that's how it was, by foot. People would come. Among many people we would go to bathe and to hear mass. There was a church here but there wasn't mass, so we would go to Pelileo. They taught [people] how to pray: the priests, the nuns, and a person called Pedro Caizabanda would also teach [people] to pray, at the church he would teach. . . . That Padre Galves spoke Quichua, he was a good priest. When I got married, too, I was in Pelileo almost a month. The nuns were there to make [us] work. Peeling sticks, weeding, spinning [wool], the nuns made us do that together. My husband and I were there together, we hadn't yet been married in the civil ceremony; all who were going to be married would go to the convent first. The nuns spoke Quichua, they would scold us saying, "How are you going to work helping your husband? You must learn." The nuns also taught us how to pray. They did everything well. When it was time for us to get married, they would cry as they sent us, saying, "Well, it's time to say goodbye. Now you all are leaving."

On the other hand, people would go to speak to the priest about those who drank too much. They would take them to the priest to be punished. One time when my husband hit [me] I went to speak to the priest. A week later, in Pelileo, he grabbed him there and in the same way he punished him. After Father Galves there was the one called Father Barrionuevo.

Manuela recollects that she turned to the Catholic priest when her husband became abusive. In her work on gender and race in nineteenth-century Ecuador, Erin O'Connor (2007:68) suggests that indigenous women who were victims of domestic violence were more likely to seek protection outside of the state court system, and that ecclesiastical courts may have provided one alternative for seeking justice. Manuela told of turning to the local priest, rather than ecclesiastical courts, to punish her husband for abusive behavior. Her story reveals one (often overlooked) aspect of the nature of the relationship between Catholic priests and indigenous actors: in this case, an indigenous woman used the priest, in the context of the doctrina, to discourage domestic violence in her own marriage.

Both these memories from elderly Salasacan women speak to the cultural production of modern religious practices that occurred as representatives of the institutional church interacted with indigenous people and their customs. The women both associate catechismal instruction with bathing in particular springs, thereby linking their religious histories to local sacred topography. Both women remember the names of early indigenous catechists who taught the others how to pray in a mixture of Quichua and Spanish. Rosa recalled the value of respect, in that younger people always greeted older people, and the older practice of serving the priests and nuns for a month while learning religious lessons and life skills as a prerequisite for being married. The obligation of serving priests or nuns is no longer practiced by Salasacans, but the memories show how much the church was a part of the emergence of modern indigenous culture.

Conclusion

Although sponsorship positions stemmed from Catholic colonial institutions, indigenous people shaped the religious celebrations and the role of sponsors to serve as mediums for sustaining indigenous cultural memory. Anthropologists working in the Andes emphasize the importance of studying rituals and social institutions as they emerged in cultural frontiers, as a result of encounters with colonial and nation-state policies, as well as the different modes of recording history and counterhistory (Abercrombie

1998b; Dover 1992:8; Rappaport 1994). The social organization and collective rituals of the Salasacans are the result of the processes that took place in the postcolonial contact zone, of the interaction of global and local histories. The evangelization project of the church began in the colonial period, but well after independence religious authorities continued their attempts to incorporate indigenous people into the Catholic faith and obligate them to conform to Eurocentric religious practices. The Salasacans, for their part, accepted many beliefs and rites of the Catholic faith but also modified them to produce their own version of an Andean Christianity. In the context of postcolonial Ecuador, indigenous individuals fought for control over their own religious lives: they appealed to Quito to have their saint's statue returned to them, they sent letters arguing for the appointment of particular festival sponsors, and they prevented a priest from carving into a sacred tree. Men wrote to the archbishop of Quito, using persuasive textual strategies to gain positions of authority in their communities. The events discussed in this chapter show how different actors in this society exercised agency and negotiated cultural conflicts; they reveal the complexity of the relationship between religion and power in Ecuador's nation-building period.

Once the nuns established themselves in Salasaca in 1945, they worked with the priests to select the festival sponsors called alcaldes. Thus began the emergence of the *rezajchicuna*, which means "ones who pray." If a man wanted to become alcalde mayor, he would have to show the nuns that he knew certain Catholic prayers necessary for the domestic ritual feasts that surround festival celebrations, funerals, weddings, and all special occasions. Therefore, a man who wanted to become alcalde mayor had to learn from previous alcaldes how to pray, and the tradition continues to this day. The prayers represent textual transculturation: they switch from Quichua to Spanish and interweave fragments from Catholic prayers with Quichua memories of the ancestors. In the next chapter, I analyze the social role of the alcaldes as sustainers of cultural memories.

CHAPTER 4

Prayer and Placemaking in the Andes

Staffholders and Cultural Memory

IN CHAPTER 3 I DISCUSSED the continued development of the institution of festival sponsorship in the early twentieth century. The focus of this chapter is how fiesta sponsors use Catholic feast-day celebrations to sustain cultural memory through two types of performance: one is recitation of old prayers and Quichua oratory; the other is movement along ritual pathways. There are several types of festival sponsorship positions in Salasaca, including *capitanes*, men who sponsor the celebration of Capitán in December, and *caporales*, men who sponsor the fiesta of Caporales in February. I will briefly discuss Caporales, because people frequently refer to this fiesta in their descriptions of sacred geography. The main focus of this chapter, however, is the role of the alcaldes—the staffholders—as sustainers of cultural memory through their performance of prayer texts and placemaking ceremonies. Alcaldes are men who volunteer to pay for music, food, corn beer (called *asua* in Quichua and *chicha* in Spanish), and cane alcohol (*trago*) used in Catholic Church–related celebrations for one year.[1] These celebrations are New Year's Day, Carnaval, Palm Sunday, Quasimodo, Corpus Christi, the Octava of Corpus Christi, and the Chishi (late) Octava of Corpus Christi. A series of private, intimate exchanges and rituals takes place around each of the public performances. These private events are as significant as the actual performances, because they involve obligatory socializing and reciprocal exchanges between members of the performance group, yet these social obligations and rehearsals have received less attention in the literature than the public performances (but see Turino 1993).

In her book *Salasaca: la organización social y el alcalde*, Eulalia Carrasco argues that the alcalde serves simultaneously to ensure internal group cohesion and to mediate relations with outside, dominant forces. Since Carrasco provides many details about festival sponsorship, I will focus here on only two aspects of alcalde performance: the rounds and the ceremonial blessings. The number of alcaldes varies from year to year depending on how many men are willing to become sponsors. Each man who desires to become a sponsor goes to the church sometime before January 1 and registers his name with the parish priest, if one is available at the time (no priest is permanently assigned to the parish), or with the Lauritas nuns. Anyone who wants to attain the position of alcalde mayor (lead alcalde) must bring a food offering (*mediano*) to the church. The alcaldes play an important role in preserving local knowledge of the landscape, and they maintain solidarity with each other and the land. I analyze the verbal knowledge and embodied knowledge of the landscape required of alcaldes. I show how the institution of alcaldes, which was originally a means for the colonial church to indoctrinate indigenous peoples, has become an important medium for sustaining indigenous cultural memory. I begin this chapter with a presentation of indigenous views on saints and Catholic feast days.

Catholic Feast Days and Saints

In chapter 2 I presented a 1907 letter from Father Barreno asking the archbishop to send a statue of the Catholic Virgin Mary to Salasaca. In Salasacan historical consciousness, however, saints came from sacred places within the earth, such as crossroads and mountains, rather than from Catholic priests.[2] According to one narrative, God made the world turn over in an earthquake, and after the earthquake the saints emerged from mountains and rocks. Each mountain or sacred place had its own Catholic saint, but "among themselves they know they are brothers and sisters." The story represents an older view of religious historical consciousness in which saints emerged independently from within the earth, especially from local topographic features such as hills and rocks. It is consistent with Salasacan constructions of local topography in which mountains and crossroads serve as places to access sacred powers.

The patron saint of Salasaca, San Buenaventura, shares characteristics with other saints of Latin American indigenous societies (see Lyons 2006:100–24). Each indigenous town has its own saint's history, often the story of who found the statue representing the saint, when, and where. That person is the founder who ensures that fiestas are celebrated in the saint's honor. The saint can cause the founder to dream, and through dreams the saint communicates his or her wishes as to where the statue should be housed. Indigenous religious historical consciousness maintains the genealogy of the family of the founder (fundador), and the position of prioste (sponsor) is passed down through inheritance from one generation to the next. Whoever is willing to inherit the position must agree to pay for a mass every year and engage in reciprocal drinking with other celebrants. María Masaquiza, who was in her sixties when I interviewed her in 2008, narrated the following genealogy of the founding of San Buenaventura:

María's great-grandfather, Vicente Masaquiza, found the saint at Cruz Pamba in the trunk of a *sigsig* (straw-bunch plant). He was the fundador (Qu. *fundador tariq*). From there, the statue of the saint was housed in the old chapel in the hamlet of Chilcapamba. Vicente Masaquiza's son Juan and daughter-in-law Espírita together inherited the position from him. The son's nickname was Juan "Curaca" (chief) because he used to make a lot of maize beer.[3] Juan "Curaca" lived to be one hundred. He passed the responsibility on to his daughter María. María passed it on to her own daughter, Rosa Jerez, who is the prioste today (*Mamamunda japin, herencia*—"She inherited it from her mother"). The narrator's own mother, Luisa "Curaca," could have taken up the position but did not want to pay for the masses and engage in ceremonial drinking. Therefore, the narrator's cousin Rosa Jerez currently maintains the fiesta of this saint, which involves once a year paying for a mass, taking the statue from the chapel to Cruz Pamba, and sharing drinks of cane alcohol at Cruz Pamba. This oral history of the founding family shows how indigenous historical consciousness relates Catholic saints to sacred places and traces the history of sponsorship through genealogical links.

According to elders I interviewed, fiestas were originally a way to give thanks to God and the earth for abundant harvests and animals, as well as to ensure future abundance of crops and livestock. Traditionally, people would honor the baby Jesus and "Tayta Vintiu" (San Buenaventura) during these events. In the following oral history, recorded in 1998 (in Quichua) Jorge, a Salasacan elder and musician, links the saints to food production, and he sets up a contrast between modern, processed foods and *granos*, the natural, locally grown foods that were the source of indigenous strength:

In the past, people worshipped Tayta Vintiu, and Mama Rosario [a female saint]. People who had a lot of granos—potatoes, corn, lentils, and also guinea pigs—they would put corn or whatever granos they had next to the saint in order to have more. Those who believed would venerate the saint and had lots of granos. People would go to Salasaca [meaning Old Salasaca, the hamlet of Chilcapamba] early in the morning and beg that the saint help [with the crops]. They celebrated the fiestas with all their faith in God, and they had lots of granos. In the past, more people went to mass. . . . Today, foods are processed, and the first *sami* [breath, essence] is removed from the food. That's why Salasacans are weaker today. In the past, one Salasacan could take on five Spaniards, because they were so strong from the nourishment of all the granos. My grandmother had a lot of granos in her harvest and wanted to sponsor a fiesta in the name of Tayta Vintiu in order to share the granos with the people. She gave a lot of maize beer, hominy, and soup to all the people, in the name of Tayta Vintiu. In the past it was like an exchange: people would have festivals, and God would give more granos.

Salasacans refer to San Buenaventura using the term *tayta*, which means "father" but is used as a respectful term for all older men. Tayta Vintiu, like many sacred entities, has his female counterpart, Mama Rosario. By worshipping at sacred sites, sponsors believe that they will be rewarded with abundant harvests and fertile livestock. Jorge also shares the widespread feeling among Salasacans that the pure, natural foods that they ate in the past gave people more energy and strength than do the rice, noodles, bread, and processed foods that people eat today. People still eat the traditional foods, of course, but these are no longer the only foods in their diets. I have heard Salasacans comment on the strength of people who live exclusively on the traditional diet of potatoes, beans, corn, and other granos (for an analysis of the meanings of foods in highland Ecuador see Weismantel 1988). Jorge used the term *sami* (a Quichua term that means "life essence," "air," or "breath") to describe the essence that is removed from processed foods. The concept of sami is significant in Andean thought, as well as among Amazonian Quichua speakers, as it embodies both personal essence and life force (Allen 1988; N. Whitten 1976).

The fiesta of Corpus Christi is one of the largest festivals sponsored by the alcaldes. Luis, an elder and former alcalde mayor, explained the festival of Corpus Christi this way:

> We Salasacans believe that God and the Virgin together, and the Virgins of this earth [*pacha*, "time-space"] together, help that we have granos; that they give corn, potatoes, and squash. They ask that the saints give rain. All of us Salasacans who believe worship in this way. The old ones used to say that the Thursday of Corpus Christi was a great day. All would meet at the church in Pelileo, all the saints. Tayta San Antonio from up in [the mountain] Teligote, Mama Nives from [the mountain] Nitón, and Tayta Vintiu from here in Salasaca all would gather together at the church in Pelileo. The people would go to Pelileo carrying the Virgin [who was] dressed in clothes, [and they would carry] oranges, limes, and corn. They would have the granos blessed [*bendiciachimun*], and return back to Salasaca with those granos. When people cleanse the guinea pig cages with plants, they can put [the plants and waste from the cages] in any crossroads, but Cruz Pamba is most significant. On Corpus Christi, when they come from down in Chilcapamba and come out on that road Calli Ñan [to Cruz Pamba] . . . [Cruz Pamba is significant because] it is a resting area there. It's a resting point on the way to Pelileo. All rest there, the alcaldes, the dancers, and the prioste.

Luis emphasizes the connection between time and space. The place called Cruz Pamba is powerful, but more powerful on certain days than on others. On Thursday of the annual Corpus Christi celebration, which coincides with the pre-Columbian solstice celebrations, the point in space intersects with the point in time to form an energy source that people can tap. Luis's mention of the specific pathway to the crossroads Cruz Pamba, along the road called Calli Ñan, is significant, for the performance is as much about tracing out ritual space as praying to God and the saints. Some Salasacans continue the practice of tucking seeds into their clothing and taking them to "make them hear mass" (*misata oyanchingabuj*). Just as taking the seeds to the Catholic mass is believed to make crops grow well, placing waste from the guinea pig cage at the sacred crossroads ensures reproduction of this source of meat.

Inauguration of New Alcaldes

The inauguration of the new alcaldes takes place at the Catholic mass on New Year's Day. In 1998 I attended the New Year's Day mass in the central plaza of Salasaca, where a visiting nonindigenous priest and the Salasacan priest, Father Ignacio, both said mass. Both spoke of the important responsibilities attached to the position of alcalde. The visiting priest spoke Spanish, and Father Ignacio, the first Salasacan to be ordained as a priest, spoke in Quichua. An ideal alcalde should serve the church and the community, and encourage people to attend mass, they concurred. After Father Ignacio spoke, he gave the staff of office to each alcalde, one by one. Starting with the alcalde mayor, each sponsor received his staff and pledged to serve the church and the people. Each alcalde kissed the staff as he received it. Father Ignacio spoke to each one. He relied on the metaphor of shepherds to sheep, telling the alcaldes to be *alli michiq* (good shepherds), and he told the people to respect the authority of the staff.

After mass, the alcaldes circled the plaza several times, then walked to a maize beer tavern in Pelileo to drink together. Every Sunday the alcaldes attend mass then drink together afterwards. Adult Salasacans remember a time when the alcaldes had certain duties to the church and the community, including cleaning the church, advising the nuns about people in their hamlets who were ill, making the priest aware of unmarried couples who were cohabiting, and rounding up children who were not attending school (Carrasco A. 1982; Corr 2003b). Although the alcalde mayor is still responsible for assisting priests and keeping up the church, many of these duties have been superseded by the alcaldes' roles as festival sponsors.

Ritual, Landscape, and Identity

One of the main duties of the alcaldes is to make the series of rounds called *muy* (also called *muyu*, from *muyuna*, "to go around"), four times a year. This involves running in line to every single Salasacan household in the parish to shake hands with a representative of the household. At each house, they say, "Praise be to God! Mothers, Fathers, may we live to see another year. Please accompany us to mass on Sundays" (Carrasco A. 1982). Although the original purpose of the rounds might have been to encourage people to attend mass, few families attend mass on a regular basis. Rather than encouraging people to go to mass, the motive for the alcaldes seems to be to establish social relations with the Salasacan people. In performing the rounds, the alcaldes trace out the boundaries of the parish. The alcaldes, through the muys, create a human line that snakes through the footpaths of the entire parish over the course of two days. They move single file, from the alcalde mayor to the last in line, who carries the whip, symbolic of his role to ensure that the alcaldes comply with their obligations, and to scare off dogs (Carrasco A. 1982:74). During the first of the four muys, the alcaldes' wives run behind them, carrying the *huanlla* (food to share) on their backs for a collective meal.

Two rules apply to the muy. The first is that all alcaldes must go barefoot. The penalty for wearing shoes to this event is that the offender is fined one liter of trago (sugarcane alcohol), which the other alcaldes collectively consume. One man's interpretation of this rule is that a sponsor should know his landscape: he should know the old pathways, and his feet must have contact with the earth so that he demonstrates his knowledge of how to run over the network of foot trails without injuring his feet on thorns. The requirement that Salasacan alcaldes make rounds ensures that the performance of this event embodies a relationship between the sponsors and their landscape, the territory of the Salasacan people.

The second rule is that each alcalde, no matter how drunk or tired he may be, must go to every single Salasacan household. As Carrasco (1982:79) reported, to skip a house would be to consider the family non-Salasacan. A man who passes out drunk during the event must pay a liter of trago for each house that he misses. This rule ensures that the performance of the muy establishes a relationship between the sponsors and the Salasacan people whom they serve. It unites the Salasacan people through a common identity. The sponsors shake hands with a representative of every single Salasacan family living in the parish, but not with non-Salasacans (*cholos*, "whites") living there.

The two rules of the muy connect physical territory with group identity through the "ritualization of concepts of space and geography" (Rasnake 1986: 667). In describing the celebration of Carnaval in Yura, Bolivia, Roger Rasnake writes, "All of the festivals sponsored by the *kuraqkuna* not only emphasize the structure of social groups but also link the multiple groupings of the social order to a conception of their physical territory. This sacralization and 'socialization' of space is an aspect of ritual language quite widespread in the Andes" (Rasnake 1986: 667). Indeed, Andean ethnic groups from Colombia to Bolivia perform ritual "possession ceremonies" by tracing the borders of their territory and pulling weeds from the earth and throwing them (Abercrombie 1998b:9; Rappaport 1994: 93). These indigenous ceremonies have roots in traditional Spanish practices for legally recognizing property rights but have become an Andean indigenous ritual expression of ethnic identity and territory.

The marking of ethnically defined space physically connects Salasacans within their territorial and social boundaries. The performance of the muy creates a characteristic of what Christopher Tilley (1994: 17) describes as existential space:

> Existential space is in a constant process of production and reproduction through the movements and activities of members of a group. . . . It is experienced and created through life-activity, a sacred, symbolic and mythic space replete with social meanings wrapped around buildings, objects and features of the local topography, providing reference points and planes of emotional orientation for human attachment and involvement. . . . Boundaries are to do with creating distinctions and marking out social oppositions, mapping social and cultural difference and Otherness.

Through the performance of the muy, the staffholders are making place; that is, through physical movement they are symbolically re-creating contact with the land and contact with indigenous families exclusively—those Salasacan people with ties to the land. As Sarah Radcliffe (1990:577) shows for the annual rounds performed during Carnaval in Kallarayan, Peru, "the ritual attempts to homogenize the villagers' identity and to emphasise its bounded territoriality." If Andean possession ceremonies originally served to mark boundaries, modernday ritual circumambulations of the community symbolically express the relationship between ethnic groups and land.

The alcaldes also trace out old, ritual pathways during the fiesta of Corpus Christi in June. Although the alcaldes sponsor a series of festivals from January through July, I will focus only on this final, and largest, celebration. In this chapter and the next, I show how this Catholic feast day is a context for sustaining the memory of sacred pathways and the genealogical memory of family groups.

The Festival of Corpus Christi

Corpus Christi is the Catholic feast day of the Body of Christ (Dean 1999; Rubin 1991). The date of its celebration depends on the Roman Catholic Church calendar but, as with many Catholic feast-day celebrations in the Andes, indigenous cyclical celebrations were merged with Catholic feast days to celebrate native cultural events such as cleaning irrigation canals, planting crops, gathering harvests, and performing animal fertility rituals (MacCormack 1991; Salomon 1986).

The Participants

Each alcalde must find his own musician, called the *maestro*, and three men who will be his dancers, called *danzantes*. The musician simultaneously plays the drum and flute while the danzantes move back and forth in a synchronized rhythm. The dancers also must each find a *catiq* ("follower," also called the *uma marca*, because he helps to carry the heavy headdress), a man who will substitute when the dancer is too inebriated to continue. The catiq should recover the hat and other personal belongings that an exhausted, inebriated dancer might lose. In social events women often take on this role of caring for the personal belongings of their husbands.

The musician, dancers, and followers each must ask a woman to accompany him. These people form the core group of participants for each sponsor. In 1998 there were eighteen of these core groups. Each group engages in reciprocal exchanges in intimate ceremonial events related to the public performance, and the sponsor refers to the participants as his sons and daughters. Similar to the way a theater group spends many long nights rehearsing together and socializing in behind-the-scenes interactions necessitated by the public performance, so festival participation brings different people into an intimate circle of those involved in the core group. The events include the rehearsal, the ceremonial delivery of the costumes, the public performance, the ceremonial return of the costumes, and the post-fiesta collective meal called *tumina*. Several Salasacan families possess the old costumes as family heirlooms, and they rent them out to the alcaldes and participants each year. Each exchange is marked by collective drinking and reciprocal meals. I will focus here on the all-night *ensayo*.

The Ensayo

Prior to the public performance, the participants gather at night for the ensayo. Although *ensayo* means "rehearsal" in Spanish, this ritual is about obligatory socializing and reciprocal exchanges rather than practice. While most people in the community are sleeping, the participants for that year's Corpus festivities stay up all night performing a ritualized exchange with one another. During many cold June nights in Salasaca, as I went to sleep I could hear the distant drumbeat in the countryside during the ensayo leading up to the fiesta. During the all-night ensayo, the group gathers at the alcalde's house for a meal, then follows the foot trails to the first dancer's house for a ceremonial meal and drinks. After some time, the group moves on to the next dancer's house and shares in another ceremonial meal, then moves on again. After feasting at the last dancer's house, they circle back to their starting point at the alcalde's house or, if the alcalde so decides, they might stop to dance at Cruz Pamba first. By this time the sun is rising, and they continue feasting and drinking at the alcalde's house for the day. The ensayo is a journey that involves travers-ing pathways together all night and returning to the starting point. The group's spatial movement connects the homes of the alcalde and dancers. I participated in this ritual twice: once in 1992 and again in 1996, when I accompanied women whose husbands were dancers. It is physically uncomfortable: it involves (for the women) long hours of sitting on the hard ground at each house, and the mountains get very cold at night. But it is part of the obligatory socializing that strengthens relationships among the participants and their families.

Public Performance

The actual performance of Corpus Christi requires a costumed display of dancing, music, and distribution of food and alcohol. At the home of the alcalde the dancers sometimes dance on the roof of the house, carrying pots, plates, and spoons. Then each alcalde with his core group walks to Cruz Pamba, where groups congregate from all sectors in the parish. Many Salasacan spectators, as well as Ecuadorian and occasionally international tourists, come to Cruz Pamba to see all the alcaldes and their core groups unite at this point. The space is crowded with dancers, and the musicians produce a cacophonous sound as each plays his instruments. The dancers circle around the cross (which is built over the hole where people place offerings) twice in a counterclockwise direction, called *alli ladomu*, which means "toward the right side," or "toward the good side."

Next they walk along the old road that leads to Pelileo, while spectators travel by bus or pickup truck. The alcaldes, musician, and dancers stop at certain named, traditional places along the road, where they dance and share cane alcohol. Most of these places no longer hold significance for the majority of Salasacan people. It is only in the fiesta of Corpus Christi that their memory is maintained. The first of the stopping points along the way is a depression in the road called Cuchinilla Pugru, "depression of cochineal (prickly pear cactus) plants." The elders say that this was the locus of good and bad souls of the deceased. The second stop is at a place called Achqu Pantión, "dog cemetery," in an area where people used to bury dogs in a large pit. Although the place no longer serves this function, each year the dancers must stop and dance at this point on their way to Pelileo, thus enacting the memory of past topography. The next stop is called Cashcabel Huatana, where the dancers stop to tie small bells around their ankles. These bells become part of the rhythm of the music as they dance. Finally, in Pelileo they go to a place called Tsontso Mati.

At the place called Zapatos Churana Pamba the dancers put their shoes on before finishing the walk and performing in the center of Pelileo. Until this time, the dancers would traditionally walk barefoot on the path between their parish and the town. In Pelileo, the dancers perform in the street and circle around the church several times as blanco-mestizo townspeople watch. A high point of the celebration is when the alcalde gives the signal for the dancers to release the doves they are holding. The doves fly up into the air above the church to the applause of the spectators. The performers drink together at a *chichería* (family-owned maize beer tavern) then return home at night.

The relationship between ethnic group territory and the neighboring blanco-mestizo town of Pelileo is reflected in the barefoot performance in Salasaca and the donning of shoes as the dancers enter Pelileo. This act indicates a connection between the contact of the bare foot with *runa*, (indigenous people's) soil and identity. In the muy, knowledge of the ancient trails and bare feet are requirements for the festival sponsors, who exclude non-Salasacan residents from their invitations to mass. One's footprint in the dirt has a powerful connection to the person. People say that those who want to perform witchcraft against another Salasacan take the dirt from the victim's footprint to the *yumbos* (Amazonian indigenous people), who know how to use sorcery. The footprint that one leaves in the dirt, then, establishes a connection between the individual and the land and, during the muy and Corpus Christi performance, distinguishes between Salasacans and non-Salasacans. Just as the barefoot performance of the muy distinguishes Salasacan from non-Salasacan people, the donning of shoes before entering Pelileo distinguishes between Salasacan and non-Salasacan territory. It also marks a distinction between a former center and periphery (before Salasaca became its own parish in 1972), between indigenous space and the space of white church and state authority.

Dancing and Drinking as Worship

It is clear that worship at points on the sacred landscape is a necessary part of the celebration for Salasacans. The ritual pathways from the Salasacan hamlet of Chilcapamba to the church in the town of Pelileo are a necessary part of the celebration of the earth and the adoration of God. Statements from Salasacans indicate that the necessary component of properly worshipping God, the Virgin Mary, and the saints is the requirement of dancing in particular spaces. The alcalde mayor of 1998 explained to me that he had to learn the journey to Pelileo, and he described the names and traditions behind each stopping place, stating, "This is the custom of the past times." This alcalde mayor was successful in gaining his position partly because he knew the name of each place where the alcalde's core group should stop along the road to Pelileo. Tilley reminds us of the power of a name to transform space into place: "Without a name culturally significant sites would not exist, but only as a raw void, a natural environment. In a fundamental way names create landscape" (Tilley 1994: 19). For this reason, most if not all crossroads in Salasaca are named, after either the roads that cross there or a person who lives nearby.

Worship through dancing at crossroads is a necessary practice during weddings as well. After the church ceremony, the wedding party must walk from the church to the home of the bride for a ceremonial meal, and then proceed from the bride's home to the groom's. The matrimonial godparents must stop to "rest" and dance at each crossroads along the way. While the godfather can stop dancing in order to serve drinks, the godmother must dance continuously (with different male partners). Thus, various celebrations enact the memory of these old pathways and stopping points through kinetic practice. Salasacan ritual events require intervals of walking, resting, and dancing along specified paths on the landscape, and people compare this activity to prayer. Luis explained to me the reason for dancing at crossroads during weddings:

> They worship at crossroads so that the bride and groom may live a good life together. So that they don't go in a bad way, they say, they make every rest [stop at every crossroads]. Since time immemorial [*desde tiempomunda*] this has held significance for them. If they don't pass well at the crossroads it is not good, they say. In the crossroads, they *must* make the rest by dancing [*Cruzeropi jursa descanso rurasha danzan*]. The deceased [in the coffin carried by pallbearers] rests in that very same place; in each good, big, crossroads.

Luis, like other Salasacans, stresses the importance of kinetic practice in culturally defined significant spaces so that the married couple will live a good life. Others told me that the bride and groom must move from the house to the church and back to the house in a counterclockwise direction, so that they will live a good life.

Prayer Texts and Memory

Ritual circumambulations along old pathways is a form of nonverbal memory. Repetition of old Quichua prayers is an important verbal performance that sustains cultural memory. Since the early colonial period, church authorities in the Andes were concerned with communicating in indigenous languages (Aymara and Quechua) and with teaching certain Catholic prayers to indigenous people. As mentioned in chapter 3, in the early twentieth century (from 1907 to 1930) priests serving in Salasaca repeatedly wrote to the archbishop of the need for a Quichua-speaking priest to give lessons to the Salasacans.

The catechism of indigenous people involved requiring alcaldes to memorize particular Catholic prayers in Spanish. Salasacans made a connection between the alcalde mayor as festival sponsor and the development of a new class of respected elder male orators, or prayer-makers, called *rezachij* (pl. *rezachijguna*). After 1945 an alcalde's learning of the Catholic prayers was overseen by the Lauritas nuns. Many of the respected staffhold-ers were illiterate and spoke limited Spanish. Nevertheless, they valued the memorization and repetition of Catholic prayers. Salasacans consider this memorized knowledge to be ancient knowledge embodied by the staffhold-ers. In a 1998 interview (translated from Quichua), Luis explained:

> This is the history that they have had, our ancestors, our grandparents and great-grandparents. They had images of San Buenaventura. So they made alcaldes, so in order to set the *mesa* [ceremonial table] they had the custom of praising San Buenaventura and praying, and remembering that it is Tayta Diositu [Dear Father God] who provides food for us. That's why they had the custom of praying, the elders from here, praising that he [God] provides food for us.
>
> The first elders, first were the old-time catechists. So then they go learning, learning, learning, then they would remain, remain, remain, little by little. In order to be an alcalde, I had to know how to pray. I had to know how to pray in the old way, and if not, one cannot be alcalde mayor, to have a ceremonial table one *must pray* praising Dear Father God, praising the alcalda [wife of the alcalde], the alcalde, Señor Buenaventura, of whom there used to be images since the times of the great-grandparents, *one must know.* The alcaldes learn, they have to be together for a whole year. For an entire year one has to go to church on Sundays. And in the past it was Thursdays and Sundays to go hear the mass, to hear what the father [i.e., priest] prays, so then one must learn what the father prays. All should learn, the wives and the alcaldes, husband and wife. So after the mass they go to rest, to bring hominy to set on the dear ceremonial table, and there they begin to pray and also to eat, after praying they eat.

Luis refers here to one of the continuing obligations of the alcaldes: that they all attend mass together every Sunday and collectively eat and drink together after mass. He emphasized that the wife of the alcalde ("alcalda") also must learn the prayers. Although in most contexts I have seen men give blessings, women also give blessings. Carrasco (1982) interviewed a woman who stood in for her alcalde husband by carrying his staff and attending mass with the other alcaldes. At wedding feasts, the bride and groom move down a receiving line from one elder male to the next as each gives a blessing, then they move into the cooking house and receive a blessing from each of the elder women.

Luis's statement that "they go learning, learning, learning . . . and they would remain, remain, remain" is a Quichua expression of the historical transmission of knowledge, in the form of memorized prayer texts, that gets passed down from one generation to the next through the system of alcaldes. Indigenous Andeans value the memorization and repetition of speech in ceremonies. For example, Andrew Orta (1999:872) reports that missionaries working among the Aymara of Bolivia used to lament the "simple" repetition of prayers, whereas the Aymara valued the ability to recite something from the *chuyma* (heart)—the site of learned knowledge associated with memory of the ancestors.

Luis is often called on to "throw" the blessing (*bendicionta shitana*) if he is present at a gathering that requires a ceremonial blessing:

> For whatever occasion when I'm around they invite me, they call me, saying "because you know a little." Because not everyone knows it. Some just don't know it. Because I understand a little of what the priest, what the nuns, prayed, what the priests have prayed, that little bit I understand. Because I don't know how to read, in my mind only I carry it. I wish I knew how to read, then I'd read some book . . . of the church, the Evangelist book or the Catholic book also, they are almost the same. But unfortunately, I can't read, and I couldn't learn now; it's too late, I'm old. I wouldn't be able to remember. But what I can do, . . . a little bit with my mind, I pray. That's right. Just like that, whenever there is a funeral wake or a wedding, they invite me, they say, "You, please, give just a little Holy Mass, Father God's little words," saying "these dear granos that God has given, everything," and the families eat together.
>
> Those old alcaldes, the nuns always taught them to pray the rosary, two hours every afternoon, in the church. That custom is lost now. The young people aren't interested. But in the past, people had more respect, they prayed with the nuns. They paid attention. So, I don't know how to read but just paying attention somehow I pray, like this; it might be a little confused but I know. I don't know everything, but I know more or less. The dear words of Father God, here, remembering somewhat, they do it. They pray.

Although older men are especially preferred to "throw" the blessing, their prayers differ. It seems that the age of the orator is more important than the content of the ritual speech. At one commemorative ritual in the cemetery during the 2002 Corpus Christi celebrations (see chap. 5), a man in his forties prayed over his mother's tomb, drew a cross in the dirt, and poured cane alcohol over the cross. Later that afternoon, he dragged an inebriated, white-haired old man to the gravesite and begged him to throw a blessing. I asked why a second blessing was needed, and his answer was that the elder men are more respected and preferred to give the blessing, even if a middle-aged adult has already given a blessing.

The prayer-makers serve as sustainers of cultural memory by re-centering Spanish texts within a Quichua oratory. I will focus on the prayers of Luis, who is respected for his knowledge of the old prayers. Luis was also considered one of the stronger fighters in the old battles of the past, when Salasaca was divided into two factions.[4] The fact that he served as alcalde mayor in the past brings him additional respect in the community. The prayers I recorded from Luis express the general performative keys of figurative language, appeal to tradition, and parallelism outlined by Richard Bauman (1984); the aesthetics of repetition with critical difference described for Quichua poetics by Harrison (1989); and the more specific aspects of Andean blessings as the product of historical processes that created this genre. As John McDowell shows, among the people of Sibondoy, Colombia, words taken from Spanish Catholic liturgy and blessings were transformed in indigenous blessings: "In fact, ceremonial speeches are cluttered with this weighty vocabulary, much of it evidently deriving from a historic moment when this speech genre developed among the indigenous elite in the colonial system" (McDowell 2000, 227).

In Salasaca, the *bendición* is a genre of verbal art spoken in the contexts of weddings, ceremonial meals, commemorative rites for the deceased, and funerary rituals. The blessing is "thrown" prior to eating the ceremonial meal, and another is said for the clearing of the table after the meal is finished. The following prayer was recited by Luis. It is the type of prayer he would say over the food on the table at a ceremonial meal. This table has woolen textiles draped over it, and cane alcohol, hominy, and maize beer are placed on top and blessed (fig. 4.1). The instructions for the alcaldes to take some hominy and begin eating are embedded within the oration.

FIGURE 4.1. The blessing for the clearing of the table after the ceremonial meal. *From left*: two dancers, two elders, the barefoot alcalde with his staff, and the maestro. The mountains Palama and Quinchi Urcu can be seen in the background.

The Blessing of the Table:

1. You all listen now, fathers, mothers, I'm going to throw a little holy blessing to all who are present, who are standing representing the young people, they are representing here babies, young people, children, and everyone [*guaguagúnama, jovenhuánama, marahuánama, tukihuánama*]. Here we are going to thank the Mother Earth [*ashpamama*], who gave us little granos, everyone is thanking, some granos, this holy blessing is thrown in the name of God whom we have chosen.

2. Now be quiet, listen to this, take off your hats, rationally now, be quiet and listen to this. The dear word of God is here, Great God, the Mother Earth [*Pachamama*] has given the granos, Virgin Mary, Mother of God, we are thankful for this. We eat these *day and night*. He takes care of us, be it *day or night*, to you all also, to the babies also,

to the elders also, to the great fathers also, the growing [adolescent] boys [*malta marahuana* = boys around age ten], for this reason, you all, we have to say thank you because he takes care of us *day and night*, so you all have to think of him [*yuyarinangichi*].

3. Our elders [*Jatun taitaguna mamaguna*] and our ancestors and ancestresses [*ñauba taitaguna ñauba mamaguna*], because they have said that one must be grateful, and one must respect what the ancestors have said: that we must live well [i.e., in peace, "beautifully," *cuidahualla*], one must not respond [when someone has offended you, *carinisha*], one must not use bad words, because the ancestors are the ones who take us forward [*ñaubucmu pushuj*].

4. I tell you all this today, to all who are seated here, to the fathers, the mothers, the young single men [*joven musuhuánama*], the girls who are almost young adults [*mara soltera tukuhuánama*, about age fourteen], the children who are growing [*malta marahuánama*, about age ten], and to young ones who by now should be conscious [twelve or thirteen years old; *ña cuintacuqhuánaga, ña cuintacunguichimi*, "as if one had just awakened," "gaining consciousness"], we are here, doing what they did before, we have also listened a little bit, we have learned a little, and from their mouths we are left, those ancestors, my grandparents, my great-grandparents had these words.

5. Now, always remembering the granos that God has given us, now the Father God gives us peas, maize, potatoes, pumpkin, squash [*quitu*], and all kinds of fruit, such as *capulí* [cherries], he gives apples, peaches, and for all this we must always be grateful and not forget him. You all, the children also, must continue always in the example of the ancestors, to always be grateful because time passes day by day, and we are becoming old, and we are disappearing, and that [the children] may continue always with the thought of continuing to thank our God for the granos that he gave us and we have to praise [him] saying:

6. Only one God like one pumpkin [*shuglla zapallu Dios*], you, Father God [*yaya Dios*], have given me to eat, give me the blessing, Mama Virgen bless me, you God, who lives in heaven, and who has given me to eat, always blessing, and for this we haven't forgotten you, because you are the Great God who lives in heaven, *yaya Dios*, in this world also you take care of everyone, *yaya Dios*, and you take care, *yaya Dios*,

and with your sami we live. Because of you we are living, because you have given me life and blood. For this reason we have always thought of you, Tayta Dios, and we want you to give us the blessing.

7. The blessing of the Father, of the son, and of the Holy Spirit, three persons only one God, like one pumpkin [*quinsa persona shuclla zapallu Dios*]. My God, you have given me to eat, thanking you we need to get our daily bread, grain by grain you all take some, all who are present here [at this point all take a bit of hominy], thank you fathers and mothers, from him, *yaya Dios*, we have taken the grain in this daily bread. Thank you.

Several features of this prayer show that it is more than just repetition of Catholic, colonial-style discourse. Rather, Salasacan blessings incorporate parts of Catholic prayers within an Andean cultural discourse. The prayer is framed from the beginning by mention of the females and males of each generation. The richness of Quichua vocabulary for referring to life stages within a generation is revealed when the orator addresses each age group in turn.

The word *Jatun taytaguna* refers to both the highly respected old men who have passed down the position of alcalde mayor and the deceased ancestors of the past, so it was translated for me as "our elders and our ancestors." Addressing the different ages of the generations present is directly linked to a major theme of this bendición: that of passing wisdom down through the generations, an appeal to tradition that will enable the people to carry on into the future.

In section 3 Luis states, "Our elders and our ancestors and ancestresses . . . and one must respect what the ancestors have said." He then states some of these words of wisdom, which are meant to generate peace among the people, with a metaphor of being carried ahead: "the ancestors are the ones who take us forward." Here he is drawing on past wisdom as a means of future survival. After that, he again addresses the males and females of all different ages, even specifying young people who are only beginning to gain awareness, and appeals to tradition again, this time specifically telling the young people to carry on the tradition: "from their mouths we are left, those ancestors. . . . You all, the children also, must continue always in the example of the ancestors, to always be grateful because time passes day by day, and we are becoming old, and we are disappearing." In this section, the importance of remembering the words of the ancestors is intermixed with the importance of remembering the food gifts that God bestows on us. In other words, he tells the audience to remember that the ancestors said to remember God. Words, "from their mouths," are vehicles for passing on indigenous knowledge. Just as the ritual circumambulations of the alcaldes express a common identity through ties to land, the prayer texts express this common identity through links to a shared past and shared ancestors. Both forms of memory reproduce Salasacan identity through links to space and time. The alcaldes serve the role of continuously recreating ethnic identity among Salasacans.

This blessing is one of the few contexts in which Salasacans refer to Mother Earth. Whereas other Andeans often refer to and honor Mother Earth (Pachamama), Salasacans rarely mention her. Luis refers to her as both Ashpamama and Pachamama in this prayer. *Ashpa* refers to earth in the sense of soil, actual land, whereas *pacha* is usually translated as timespace. Luis's references to Mother Earth in this blessing are examples of textual transculturation. Part of the Catholic indoctrination of indigenous communities involved teaching them to say blessings, and in particular to memorize the Our Father and Hail Mary. Here, the well-respected prayer-maker uses bits and pieces of those Catholic prayers in a process of "recentering of text by metonymic substitution" (Bauman and Briggs 1990:75). Lines such as "our daily bread" stand for the Catholic prayer Our Father. But Luis also expresses fundamental concepts in Andean cosmology: Mother Earth and sami. In section 6 Luis mentions sami, the life essence, as one of the gifts from God. I have already mentioned that the Quichua term *sami* refers to life force and personal essence. As will be seen in chapter 6, the concept of sami is referred to in people's explanations of shamanic powers and healing. In this prayer, Luis praises God for giving people life, blood, and sami.

To summarize, the principal duties of the alcaldes revolve around festival sponsorship, but the system of festival sponsorship itself is a vehicle for the transmission of knowledge, both verbal and kinetic. Through the muy, alcaldes physically connect the Salasacan people to the land, and during rehearsals and festivals, their dancers stop to dance at every crossroads. Furthermore, alcaldes should know the names of the old sacred places between Salasaca and Pelileo, and they should know what Salasacans consider to be the old-time prayers. Although these prayers are a product of colonization, Salasacans have re-centered them within a Quichua oratory that stresses indigenous ancestors and a common memory of a shared ancestry. Alcaldes must be skilled orators and knowledgeable of the landscape, and ideally they should also have some knowledge of Salasacan history. The fiesta sponsorship system requires new candidates for the position of alcalde mayor to seek out knowledgeable elders and learn the blessings and the ritual pathways and stopping points. The system of sponsorship, then, ensures transmission of knowledge from one generation to the next.

Caporales

The fiesta called Caporales links sacred pathways, the baby Jesus, and Salasacan livelihood. It is a mobile fiesta, usually celebrated in early February, in honor of the baby Jesus. The men who volunteer to sponsor the fiesta must ask other men to perform the role of *negros*, that is, Afro-Ecuadorian soldiers. For this, the performers smear black soot on their faces, wear helmets, and carry swords. More than one Salasacan man claimed to have been "tricked" into the obligation to take on the role by accepting a shot of cane alcohol from the sponsor. A common story is that the sponsor offers a drink to the prospective performer, and after the drink is accepted and consumed, the sponsor says, "Good! So you will perform for me." Once the drink is accepted, the person cannot refuse. The caporal also must ask other people to commit to playing the role of *doñas*, traditionally boys dressed as women who dance with the black soldiers. One of these, called the *ñuñu* (a central Andean Quechua term for "wet nurse"), carries a baby made of bread on his or her back and dances with the caporal. I observed this fiesta in 1992, 1998, and 2008. In the 1990s, the role of doña was still being played by boys who would dress as women for the fiesta. By 2002, I learned that many young men and boys no longer wanted to fulfill this role, and they were replaced by girls.

The term *caporal* was used in other parts of Latin America to refer to the black administrator, labor boss, or slave master. In the seventeenth-century sweatshop of Pelileo, the caporales were the black workers who were ordered to assist in the punishment of indigenous workers. A 1666 report stated that the Indians were "held to the ground, with two hands, by their blacks, whom they call caporales, and they punish them with whips made of cowhide" (AGI/S 1666-11-15). But this is not the meaning that the "black" characters have for Salasacans. Most Salasacans say that they dress up as black soldiers for Caporales because that is the tradition. Others relate the fiesta to the Liberal Revolution (1895), when Eloy Alfaro's army, with its Afro-Ecuadorian coastal soldiers, passed through the highlands offering benefits to indigenous people who joined the revolution. For others it holds religious significance: the men dress up and perform in order to honor the baby Jesus, and they believe that God will reward the caporal (sponsor) with abundant crops and livestock.

The actors pretend to be sexually aggressive, making lewd comments to female spectators (both indigenous and white) and sometimes groping women they catch off guard (see also Chango and Jerez 1995). There is room for improvisation. Some men told me that when they perform they shout out, "I'm from Esmeraldas [coastal Ecuador]. I'm passing through on my way to the *oriente* [Amazonian Ecuador] to work in petroleum. What beautiful women they have here in Salasaca!" Others also claim to be migrant workers from different parts of the coast. The caporal, *negros*, and doñas move along the old ritual pathways to Cruz Pamba, where they dance together and circle the crossroads, distributing food and maize beer. Before the performance, the elders bless the performers. One man who has played the role of *negro* several times told me about his first time performing: "I was really nervous. My mother gave me the blessing before I left the house. She said, 'Come back safe and sound, don't fight,' and she blessed me. I was scared about performing, but then I had a shot of cane liquor and I got up the courage. Once I drank, I just ran! I ran shouting all the way to Cruz Pamba and I didn't feel tired."

Sponsoring a fiesta is extremely costly, and for a few years in the mid-1990s, Caporales was not celebrated. People said it had "died out," but by 1998 men were again volunteering to serve as caporales. In 2008, some of the sponsors were return migrants. One had worked in Spain for several years. The fiesta had become more elaborate: at night, in the central plaza of Salasaca, each sponsor set up a stage with a (white-mestizo) band and dancers. I was surprised by this new spectacle: as Salasacans dressed in warm, woolen clothing crowded the central plaza, scantily clad blanca-mestiza women danced on the stages like female dancers seen on Latin American variety shows do. But this spectacle was an addition to the older, more traditional aspects of the celebration of Caporales. This evolution is typical of the trends I have seen in Salasacan festivities in the 1990s. Weddings and fiestas include the old-fashioned Salasacan tunes, played on the violin and drum. Late at night, the hosts of such events often hire a mestizo disc jockey to blast popular dance music in the patio, often accompanied by strobe lights and a fog machine. This trend adds to, but does not replace, the older forms of celebration.

The fiesta of Caporales, like Corpus Christi, has private events that bring the participants together before and after the public performance. A year after the performance, the old caporal reassembles his participants to hold a funeral for the bread baby that was carried by the ñuñu during the previous year's performance. Hence, while the new caporales are celebrating with their performers, the previous year's performers reunite to bury their "baby." There is no single Salasacan explanation for this rite, but it serves to unite the people, remind them of the traditions of their ancestors, and contemplate death and resurrection.

The group puts a lot of effort into the funeral. The caporal pays a man in the community to build a child-sized coffin. At night, the deceased baby is named and baptized by a prayer-maker. The baby is really two babies joined together: one male and one female. There is some variation in the naming of the babies: some people told me the babies are named after the sponsor and his wife, and they represent the child of the sponsors. In the bread-baby funeral I witnessed, however, the babies were named Manuel and Manuela, after the name Emmanuel, to honor the baby Jesus. If the baby originally represented the Christ child, Salasacans gave a female component to the figure, in accordance with Andean patterns of gender complementarity.

After the naming ceremony, a wake is held at the home of the caporal. The participants bring candles and hold a vigil near the coffin, where an elder says several Catholic prayers. They play the dice game that is associated with funeral wakes (see chap. 5). Sometimes the caporal will pay for a Catholic mass, and the pallbearers (the former "*negros*") carry the coffin to the church, where the priest says a mass for the child. In a case observed by Peter Wogan (2004:114), the priest went to the home of the sponsor to say mass. The Catholic mass is significant because it shows how indigenous people bring the officiant of the Catholic mass, and the liturgy, into their own ritual. Afterwards, musicians play the traditional violin and drum tunes associated with child wakes, and the pallbearers carry the coffin to the home of the caporal for burial. In the burial I observed in 1998, the pallbearers dug a grave in the patio, and an elder gave a ceremonial speech in which he emphasized the memory of the ancestors who practiced the same tradition and the reciprocal sharing of food among the participants. He emphasized the hard work of the caporal and reminded everyone that, like the deceased bread baby, our flesh and bones die but our souls live on. He prayed for the female bread baby, the collective "sister" Manuela, and the caporal's wife cried intensely for her "daughter."[5] Then they buried the coffin and placed flowers on the grave.

The fiesta of Caporales reveals two interesting aspects of Salasacan ritual that will be further explored in the next chapter. One is ritual intertextuality in Salasaca: the way in which Salasacans insert one ritual performance into another; in this case, a wake and funeral mass are inserted into the fiesta by the previous year's participants. Bauman and Briggs (1990:75) refer to this type of re-centering as "blended genres." The other aspect is ritual transformation through parody. People told me that the black soldiers protect the caporal from getting trapped in purgatory in the afterlife (see chap. 8). Although the indigenous actors embody and disembody the character by smearing their faces with black soot, putting on a soldier's uniform, and carrying a sword, the character exists in the afterlife to protect the soul of the sponsor (see also Wogan 2004:80). Although parody is a common aspect of rituals, in Salasaca parodies can effect a religious transformation. By asking men to parody Afro-Ecuadorian soldiers in this life, the sponsor can save his soul in the afterlife.

Conclusion

Through narrative and ritual, Salasacans re-center Catholic symbols and texts to sustain local cultural memory. Saints' genealogies locate sacred powers within local topography, and traditions are maintained within Salasacan family descent groups. The institution of alcaldes ensures that memory of old prayers and pathways is sustained through generational links between alcaldes. Finally, by holding a Catholic funeral mass for the bread baby, the Salasacans involve the priest in their own rituals. Caporales makes use of intertextuality and parody to realize a ritual transformation (protection of the soul after death).

The fiesta of Corpus Christi, based on the Catholic feast day of the Body of Christ and pre-Columbian solstice celebrations, also serves as a context for performing memory acts. In addition to enacting historical memories through the traversing of old pathways, Salasacans use Corpus Christi as the context for enacting genealogical memory by re-enacting funeral rites for deceased loved ones. In the next chapter I discuss parody and ritual intertextuality in the rituals surrounding death in Salasaca, including the commemorative rites for the dead that take place during the June Corpus Christi celebrations. Death rituals prominently reflect religious transculturation, and the rites are a cultural form of expressing kinship and social relations.

CHAPTER 5

Life Lessons at a Time of Death

AUGUST 1, 2002: I was standing outside the International Arrivals area at the airport in Quito, after a brief visit to the United States. I was waiting for Anita to meet me there, and we would ride the bus back to Salasaca together. She should have been easy to spot, as the Salasacan clothing is distinctive. After waiting for some time, I finally found Anita's two daughters, with their grandfather and two aunts, who both carried their babies on their backs. We hugged and laughed at how they had been searching for me outside the Domestic Flights area. But I wondered why Anita had not come to meet me as she had planned. So I asked her sixteen-year-old daughter: "Where's your mother?"

"Oh, she couldn't come. She was drinking yesterday."

Salasacans don't drink alone, and Anita drank only when there was a special occasion. I wondered what was going on.

R.C: What was the occasion?

M.: I don't know.

R.C.: Well, was it a wedding?

M.: No.

R.C.: Baptism?

M.: No.

R.C.: Did she go to someone's funeral? Did anyone die?

M.: No.

R.C.: Well, who did she drink with?

M.: I don't know.

Of course, she *did* know, but these girls had already learned when to discuss something and when to wait and let someone else explain what was going on. I would have to hold my curiosity during the three-and-a-half-hour bus trip south of Quito, through the rural mountain towns, to Salasaca. When we arrived in the evening, Anita was sitting by the fire in her small cooking house. As we sat in the smoke-filled room, by the warmth of the fire, she explained:

There is an elderly couple that lives yonder. They don't have any surviving children. They came by yesterday and invited me to their house to eat. I didn't know what they wanted, and I asked my friend Gladys to go with me. When we got there, they said, "We have land and a cow, but we don't have any children, and we are getting too old. You have a lot of children. If you feed our cow every day, take care of the land, and go to the mingas for us, we'll leave the land to you when we die." So I agreed, and then we all drank together to celebrate the agreement.

It was a good deal for Anita, for she had six children and not much land of her own. A hardworking woman, she was willing to get up early to feed and milk the cow, leaving some milk for the couple and taking some for her children. One day, upon seeing the older woman walking along the path, Anita's children greeted her as "grandmother." Knowing that I wouldn't understand, the six-year-old daughter explained to me, "We call her grandmother now." The fictive-kin relationship they had created extended to ritual duties. When a relative of the elderly man's died, Anita helped the old woman fulfill her ritual obligation as a *cachun* ("daughter-in-law" or "woman related by marriage") by preparing the "daughter-in-law porridge" for the funeral. I was surprised at this; not only was Anita receiving land like a daughter and were her children referring to the couple as grandparents, but Anita helped the old woman fulfill her ritual obligation to the old man's family. I asked Anita's husband (half-jokingly) if, when the old man or woman died, he would provide the dice for the funeral game *huayru*, just like a "real" son-in-law would. "Of course I will," he answered in all seriousness. Anita then told me, "That's what they said when they offered me the land. They said 'We'll give you the land, but you bury us [*pambachun*, i.e., give us a proper/good funeral] when we die.'"

A few years later Anita had a falling-out with the couple when she was unable to lend them money at a time when they needed it. Nevertheless, this story illustrates one event through which I came to learn the important links between kinship and death rituals. Indeed, it was at times of death that I learned who was related to whom by blood, by marriage, and by associations based on nurturance. When an individual dies, the family members related by blood wear special brown "mourning hats" (fig. 5.1). Those who do not own the hats must rent them from another

FIGURE 5.1. Gathered outside the cemetery gate for the funeral of Manuel
Jiménez. The family members wearing mourning hats are *(from left)*:
Rosa Manuela Jiménez, Lidia Jiménez, Violeta Masaquiza Jiménez, José
Jiménez, Francisca Jiménez (and baby Esteban), and Zoila Pilla. Notice the
daughters-in-law's chumbis (embroidered belts) wrapped around the coffin.

family. Except for the deceased's spouse relatives related through marriage do not wear the mourning hats. However, the sons-in-law (*masha*)
and daughters-in-law (cachun) have special roles and obligations in the
events of the wake and post-burial rites. Thus the death of an individual
throws underlying kinship structures into relief for ritual expression of
social relations. The presence or absence of the mourning hat is a public,
symbolic marker of one's relationship to the deceased.

Death rituals often express some of the most fundamental, underlying religious concepts of a society. This chapter shows several aspects
of Salasacan religiosity as expressed in death rituals. First, through rituals Salasacans demonstrate the value of kinship and social relations, as
social roles fall into place along specific lines. Second, Salasacans use
ceremonial games, parody, mimesis, and intertextuality to enact religious

transformations. The mimesis includes manipulation of Catholic symbols and texts in order to properly send souls to the afterlife. Third, people actively commemorate the deceased years later by repeating the same rites they performed at the time of the person's death. The purpose of this chapter is to show how Salasacans honor and commemorate their deceased loved ones through rituals. Death rituals involve the re-centering of Catholic texts and rites to sustain indigenous genealogical memory. Salasacans use ritual intertextuality—the insertion of all or part of one ritual into another—to sustain the memory of deceased loved ones and to connect the death of an individual to the collective rituals of the community. I will now describe the funeral rites in the order in which they are performed.

The Wake

It is said that when people visit various places, they leave their soul (or part of the soul) at each place. At the moment of death, all the souls from all the places a person has visited in his or her lifetime come back and unite with the person, and only at that moment does he or she stop breathing.

The death of an individual requires five days of observances by family (both consanguineous and affinal relatives), friends, and neighbors. The family holds the wake on the first night after death. During the wake the family of the deceased must feed all the attendants, and each attendant should bring a candle or money for a candle. The coffin is placed on the front porch of the house and is surrounded by candles, flowers, and crosses. If the deceased is a single young adult, the tradition is for the family to "marry" the deceased to a fowl of the opposite sex—a rooster for a young woman or hen for a young man. The family asks a couple to serve as matrimonial godparents. They "marry" the deceased, making the hand touch the wing of the bird. People have told me that the fowl stays on or near the coffin, like a true spouse (see also Jerez Caisabanda 2001:57). After the burial, the family or godparents keep the fowl until it dies naturally, then they bury it in the cemetery. This ritual performance ensures that young adults do not go into the afterlife single, but as part of a gendered pair, in accordance with Andean principles of duality and complementarity. At a wake for a sixteen-year-old girl tragically killed in a landslide during a minga, I saw the white rooster-spouse walking around the patio during the vigil. Money was attached to it, secured with colored ribbons.

In the patio, men and boys play games while women and girls watch and receive food. The reason women and children do not play the men's games is that they involve roughhousing that would be inappropriate when directed at women and children. For example, in the game called "the rooster" men line up and, one by one, jump off the roof of the house while holding a live chicken. They land in a pile of burning branches. Another man (some say the son-in-law of the deceased) stands with a branch or belt to beat them and make them keep moving, one by one. When I asked my friend Lorenzo if the men burn their feet when they land in the fire he said "No. It's that we get out right away. Why would we be standing there in the fire?" Clearly, I had asked a stupid question. This game is becoming less common now that most Salasacan homes are built of cement blocks with metal roofs than it was in the past, when people had straw houses. In fact, while men explained many different games to me, I only ever saw two performed: one was the boys' enactment of a fiesta, which I observed once, the other was huayru, which is played at every (non-Protestant) wake.

Mimicking Fiestas at the Wake

Boys sometimes put on a performance to imitate adult fiestas. This is part of the tradition of funeral wakes, but the decision to perform is spontaneous, and it is not done at every wake. With the exception of huayru, all games are optional and voluntary, but when played, the games contribute to the overall funeral ritual. At any given wake, boys organize among themselves, decide which fiesta they will enact, and decide on the roles of the participants. As with all games, the family of the deceased rewards the players with the corn-flour soup called *uchu*.

Children's games at funeral wakes, although voluntary, make a contribution to adult religious ritual. The parody of adult sacred play in the form of fiestas reflects the intertextuality characteristic of Salasacan expressive culture, in which a ritual from one context is inserted into the ritual performance in a different context. In the case of a wake, a play frame is inserted into the somber occasion of a death. I view the child's play at wakes as characteristic of Salasacan rituals, which cannot always be defined as "sacred" versus "secular." Death rituals are serious, and the children's performance of a fiesta during a wake, while humorous, is taken seriously by adults.

Children's imitation of adult fiestas is just one type of ludic activity that people perform at wakes. It raises the question of why people choose to insert games into the otherwise sad, dangerous, liminal event of someone's death. In Salasaca, the fiesta is the preeminent social act; it brings the community together year after year, in reciprocal exchanges with each other. Fiestas are also religious performances, bringing God, the saints, and the Earth Mother into reciprocal exchanges with humans. The performance of a mock fiesta at a wake expresses the idea that despite the death of an individual, the social life of the community will continue. The children who play-act fiestas today may be sponsoring them tomorrow. Although some children want simply to play, not actually to perform like adults, others will grow up to continue the tradition. But the performance at the wake is not so much a rehearsal for future roles as a parody of current social roles, and parody—even humorous parody—is a significant aspect of sacred rituals in many cultures (Babcock 1996; Drewal 1992). While many have described the relationship between religion and play in western civilizations in the past (Huizinga 1955; D. Miller 1970; Sutton-Smith 1997), and anthropologists have discussed the sacred meanings of ludic activities for non-western societies (Babcock 1996; Drewal 1992; Turner 1979), the interrelationship between religion and play is still difficult for many outsiders to comprehend. For Salasacans, humor and play do not undermine the sacredness of rituals. Children's wake games are ritually sanctioned play that contribute to the overall success of the wake.

The fiestas most commonly enacted are the alcalde-sponsored fiesta of Palm Sunday, the alcaldes' rounds, the fiesta of Capitán, and the fiesta of Caporales. Adult men whom I interviewed enthusiastically described the types of games that boys and men play at wakes. According to Alfredo

> There is the game *capitán*. At night, the boys discuss it among themselves. They arrive mounted on burros or horses, dressed as [the fiesta characters] *loas*, soldiers, *pajes*, and the capitán. They say [to the owner of the burro], "Lend it to us for a little while." Or sometimes the owner is at the wake, and they just take it. When they come riding into the patio, the owner will say, "Even my burro has come to the wake!"

Another game is alcaldes. The boys take *carrizo* stalks and peel the leaves off. They go from house to house and leave the branches at the houses, saying they are leaving palm fronds. Then they return to the wake and ask for uchu.

Alfredo focused on the various fiesta characters that boys imitate from the fiesta of Capitán, and the props that they gather for their performance. He also described the imitation of the Palm Sunday celebration in which the alcaldes fulfill their obligations by providing palm leaves for everyone in the community. One of the more humorous aspects of gathering props for the performance occurs when the boys "borrow" a burro from a neighbor in the middle of the night, often without the neighbor's knowledge. The same humorous activity was mentioned in the following interview with a man named Lorenzo and his sister. Lorenzo recalled

> We used to play alcalde . . . we would get carrizo stalks, taking off the leaves. We used to get together as boys, maybe eight, ten of us, as many as we wanted. Sometimes we would go all the way down by the river to get the stalks. And we'd come to the house where the wake was being held, made up like alcaldes. With a carrizo stalk, like a staff, we would walk around where the deceased was, around the coffin. Then with the leaves of the carrizo we would give them out to other attendants at the wake, saying they were palm fronds. That's how we used to play alcalde. We also played [the fiesta] Rey, riding a burro. At night we would get on the burro. We'd put a crown on the boy mounted on the burro, and we would wrap shawls around the burro. The other boys would be the negros [performers as Afro-Ecuadorian soldiers], six on this side, six on that side, using shawls as part of the costume. But the one playing *rey* [king] rides in on the burro.

Lorenzo's older sister joined in at this point, recalling a time when a child "borrowed" someone's burro to perform at a wake: "They were playing Capitán, and they were going around taking burros from wherever, and the woman who owned the burro went around saying, 'Ay! Someone stole my burro! I've been robbed.' Then someone told her, 'No, it was Marcelino who took it.' All the boys had gotten together [to perform at the wake]."

They both laughed as they recalled the incident, and Lorenzo's sister suggested that Marcelino, who is now a grown man, derived his nickname,

"Burro Thief," from the misunderstanding. (See Wogan 2004:54 on the Salasacan practice of assigning nicknames to adult men.) Lorenzo also described the gathering of props, to the extent of going to the river to gather the carrizo stalks. In his recollection, the stalks were used for a different purpose than imitating the Palm Sunday fiesta: they represented the alcaldes' staffs of authority, and the child-alcaldes circled the deceased in the coffin as they imitated the movement of the sponsors. Rey is related to the fiesta of Caporales, and the children used shawls to dress up a burro the way they are dressed up with cloth for this fiesta.

When I asked Luis, an older man knowledgeable in the community's history, about the child's version of the "alcaldes," he explained

> First, one is in the corner made up like a priest. All the boys gather carrizo stalks, making little pieces, sticks or whatever. Then they give it to the "priest" but they decide outside which one will be the priest, the children themselves decide. They decide, saying, "You should be the priest and give the staffs of office." So they give it there. They continue receiving the staffs, and they say, "We're doing alcaldes." They make the rounds from house to house, just like the alcaldes, to each house. They do this the night of the wake—around midnight, or ten or eleven at night, or at one in the morning, according to the hour at which they want to play. The very night of the wake they make the rounds from house to house, giving out branches. In that way, *as if they were the alcaldes, carrying out the same obligations* [my emphasis]. They are there to shake hands [with the owners of the houses]. The neighbors are sleeping but they do it. So they go one round, just like that they come, the alcaldes. Made up like alcaldes, the children. With their staffs of carrizo stalk, one has to make it out of a stalk. They give these to each one, they come bringing it to the wake. One returns with a stalk. So one has to distribute it at the time of the wake. Like on Palm Sunday. Then we say "huayruchu" or "alcalde uchu." They are accustomed to ask for it. Then, [the family of the deceased] in turn, has to feed them.

Luis noted the relationship between the reference to the corn-flour soup and the type of game played: although the family of the deceased serves the same uchu to the players, in the context of the huayru game it is called *huayruchu*. If the family is rewarding boys who played alcaldes, it is called alcalde uchu. The change of the name of the food in each context indicates its symbolic function in ritual; it serves as a reciprocal exchange of food for the performance of a particular game.

In Luis's description, he refers to the January 1 inauguration of the new alcaldes during the Catholic mass, when the priest distributes a staff of office to each alcalde, symbolizing his authority in the community. According to Luis, boys enact this event by choosing one child to be the "priest," and they involve the sleeping neighbors in their play-acting. The boys imitate the muy, or the rounds that the alcaldes perform four times a year, when they go from house to house, shaking hands with a representative of the household and encouraging people to come to mass with them on Sundays (see chap. 4). On the night of the wake, neighbors not in attendance are drawn into the children's performance of the mock muy.

Luis also emphasized the children's autonomy in the performance, stating "the children themselves decide" upon the roles to be performed. He also elaborated on the mimetic aspect of the performance when he said "as if they were alcaldes, carrying out the same obligations." The statements from adults indicate that child's play is an autonomous activity in which the child actors take care to imitate the fiestas that bring the community together year after year.

At one wake in 1993 I witnessed the performance of the fiesta of Capitán, usually celebrated in November or December. The boys came riding in on burros, representing the adult male actors who dress as soldiers and ride horses for the fiesta. One boy played the role of the loa, the child who gives a speech and presents the sponsor and performers. As the boys enacted this fiesta in the space of the patio where the corpse was laid out in its coffin, the men listened intently. A couple of men occasionally corrected the loa during his speech, and a friend later told me that this was a disorganized performance. Boys who are better organized, he said, take more care to imitate the costumes of the actual fiesta participants. After the performance, the "owners," the family of the deceased, brought the boys their uchu.

During this particular performance, the parody of the fiesta extended to include the role of the women who follow the male participants and receive their portion of food in calabash bowls. The family of the deceased asked the boy actors who their female "followers" were, and each boy selected a girl or, in one case, a grandmother, who subsequently received a portion of the uchu. Therefore, although the performance was organized by the boys, the adults hosting the wake contributed with their innovation of the role-playing. Since the play fiesta was an imitation of adult roles, I later interviewed one of the boys and asked if he really wanted to perform as a "soldier" in the fiesta when he grows up. "No," he replied. "They want you to drink a lot, and I don't want to get drunk." This child wanted to limit his festival obligations to ritual play.

Wakes are a fundamentally religious activity. The wake is a ritual observance in honor of the deceased, meant to pay respect to and appease the soul. Since adults sanction children's parodies of fiestas during wakes, in this context children's play is constitutive of collective religious ritual.

The Huayru: Making Souls Happy

While the fiesta parodies and other games are voluntary, and may or may not occur at a wake, the dice game called huayru must be played at every wake. The huayru is an elongated six-sided die carved from an animal bone. The Salasacan game piece is very similar to pre-Columbian objects that archaeologists have found in Ecuador, and versions of funerary dice games have been reported throughout South America.[1]

Several families own a huayru die, and at the death of an individual, the son-in-law of the deceased must rent it from one of those families. If the deceased has more than one son-in-law, it is the eldest's responsibility. If the deceased does not have a son-in-law, the obligation passes to another in-married male, such as the granddaughter's husband (nieto masha), sister's husband (pani masha), or niece's husband. Anthropologists working in other parts of the Andes have described the special roles of the son-in-law (and, by extension, other in-married males) during funerals and other rituals, such as house-raising (Lambert 1977; Mayer 1977). Salasacans explain that the responsibility falls to the son-in-law because he is "like a son," and yet he is clearly distinguished from a son because he does not wear a mourning hat like his wife and the deceased's other blood relations. Perhaps because they are related to the deceased through marriage, in-laws carry out special responsibilities to prove their devotion to the deceased.

For example, one elder stated that the son-in-law rents and presents the game piece at the wake "for his wife," while the daughter-in-law makes separate portions of *cachun api* (porridge) on behalf of her husband and each unmarried son. The rituals and symbols both incorporate affines and distinguish them from blood relatives.

Family members related to the deceased by blood (those who wear the mourning hats) do not participate in funeral games. When the huayru game starts, a man will give the first toss, and all see what number it lands on. Then he gives the die to each man in turn to throw, and if it lands on a lower number than the previous throw, the first thrower slaps the second on the back of the hand very hard. If it is higher, the second player slaps the first on the hand. Men visibly wince in pain after being slapped, and another man, who is passing out shots of cane alcohol at the wake, will come and say "Here have some 'blood' (*yahuar*), to calm you." The cane alcohol is figuratively referred to as "blood" in this context, and drinking it is said to calm the red, stinging hand. If the huayru lands standing upright, rather than on one side, all the players beat the thrower on the back. Salasacans use the onomatopoeic term *lutsquinucusha* to describe the way the men slap each other, and their expression of pain is part of the humor of the game (see Waskosky 1992 for an excellent linguistic analysis of the description of this game).

If the huayru lands on 5, a special number, the men all yell "Mama Cinco!" The significance of the number 5 is a common feature of this game in various regions, and the Incas referred to the game as both "huayru" and "pishca," meaning "five." In some ethnographic and historical contexts the game was associated with a ceremony held five days after the burial (Brownrigg 1989).

If the huayru piece is lost, the son-in-law must pay a fine. Sometimes men will hide it, and the masha has to find it. I once found it lying in the dirt path on my way home from a wake. As I was returning to give it back, people told me that I couldn't just give it to the masha, I was supposed to charge him for returning it. Huayru is played all night, and even the next day, after the Catholic mass. As the mourners, guests, and pallbearers carry the coffin along the road to the cemetery, they stop at crossroads to rest, distribute store-bought wine, and play huayru. Crossroads are powerful places in Salasacan cosmology, and one large crossroads on the way to the cemetery is called *alma samana crucero*, the "corpse-resting-crossroads." Crossroads symbolize trial, risk, chance, and transition as well as mediation of opposing forces. Salomon (2002:3) shows that in other parts of the Andes the ritual game is not limited to funerary contexts but rather expresses important social and political passages. In Huarochirí, the game is played during the transition from the old year to the new and marks the change in political authorities. In Salasaca the playing of the game of chance at the place where paths cross emphasizes these symbolic meanings of passage and transition in a context of the uncertainty of life and death.

Although huayru might have its roots in determining the distribution of the deceased's property or divining the will of the deceased, none of the people I interviewed gave such explanations. Only one person I interviewed gave an explanation; he said that by playing huayru the mourners are "making the soul happy" (*almata cushiyachilla*). This elder's explanation indicates that the ludic wake activities have the transformative capacity to appease the soul of the deceased. The word he used, *cushiyachilla*, makes use of the Quichua affixes *-ya* (becoming) and *-chi* (causative) and indicates an ongoing process as the game is played (Waskosky 1992). The players cause the soul to become happy during the course of the night's games. To please the soul of the deceased may be an underlying motive for the other games as well.

The Burial

The wake lasts all night. At dawn (or anytime after 2 a.m.), the daughters-in-law of the deceased and other women related to the deceased through marriage (subsumed by the term *cachun*), bring the attendants a type of red corn-flour porridge (cachun api) made from the flour of red, blue, and purple maize. Cachun api is the same porridge as *puka api*, which is served during the collective rituals for the dead during the Day of the Dead on November 2. In the context of funerals, it is called cachun api because the women related to the deceased through marriage are obligated to contribute it on behalf of the male consanguineous relatives. A woman prepares one ceramic vessel (pondo) or bucket of cachun api for her husband, and one for each unmarried son. Married sons contribute cachun api prepared by their wives. Just as the son-in-law rents the huayru for his wife, the daughter-in-law prepares the ritual drink for her husband and adult sons related to the deceased.

Later in the morning, after consuming large quantities of the porridge, the family prepares to carry the coffin to the church for mass. The daughters-in-law are obliged to lend their embroidered belts (*chumbi*) to wrap around the coffin (see fig. 5.1). The pallbearers carry the coffin once around the house, so that the deceased circles the space of the living one last time. This is an emotionally charged farewell, as family members follow the coffin around the house and some cry out the name of the deceased. The attendants take the coffin to the church, where the pallbearers place it on a stand in front of the altar. The priest says mass for the deceased, including Catholic hymns and prayers for the soul to go to heaven. From the church, the party moves on to the cemetery, stopping at each crossroads to "rest," share drinks, and for the men, play huayru until the cemetery gate is reached. Once they enter the cemetery, they no longer play. Friends and neighbors dig the grave, which takes some time. Market women and men from the city come to sell food, ice cream, and drinks outside the cemetery, because digging the grave can take hours in the hot sun.

Occasionally, the gravediggers come across bones from a previous burial. These bones can offer protection to the living. Some say that those who take bones from the cemetery to keep at their homes are protected from thieves because the bones converse at night. If the grave diggers encounter a previous burial, they might take dry scrapings from inside the cranium, which is also called *pilche*, like the calabash bowls that women carry to fiestas. These dry scrapings are mixed in a cup of sugarcane alcohol and those who choose to do so consume it. As is typical of ceremonial drinking, all drink from the same cup. The *ñutcu cuta* ("brain dust") is thought to prolong life by protecting its consumers against witchcraft and fear. Having drunk the scrapings from the cranium, the person's soul is said to transform, appearing as many souls of the dead (sometimes described as having the form of moths) and making it impossible for enemies to ensorcel because the sorcerers cannot "catch" the soul of the intended victim. Some men explained to me that "drinking from the cranium" gives force and courage, and attributed the long lives of some elders to this consumption. However, it can also be dangerous. People told me that drinking dust from the cranium causes one to have particular dreams, and it changes the way people behave when they engage in drinking, causing them to become more easily agitated.

Death and Emotion

Culture mediates the ways in which people express grief. Ritual prescribes how and in what way mourners show their emotions (Geertz 1973), but obviously people's feelings are not limited by ritual rules. After one funeral, when all the rituals had been completed, I was speaking with the daughter-in-law at the home of the deceased. "Come look," she whispered to me. "She's crying." And we quietly watched the widow, sitting alone on her porch, sobbing to herself. However, the most open expressions of grief that I have seen occur at the moment of burial.

People place money, sometimes food, and calabash bowls in the coffin with the deceased. Women are buried with their distaffs, wool, and spindles, as the woman's soul will be sad if she leaves her spindle behind. Throughout the time of my fieldwork in the 1990s, women always walked around spinning wool by hand (except on Sundays), and my friend Espirita taught me how to spin (see fig. 5.2). After the pallbearers lower the coffin into the grave, they remove the chumbis from the coffin and return them to the daughters-in-law. All remove their hats, and a rezachij bestows the blessing. As family members throw dirt on the coffin a woman, or women, wail poetically. The first time I heard a woman wail at a burial, I thought she was singing, but I later learned that Salasacans do not classify the high-pitched, poetic lament as singing but rather as crying. For a man, they might say, "My dear little neighbor. You are gone. Who will weave clothes for your family now? Who will till the fields?" In his 1934 novel *Huasipungo*, the Ecuadorian author Jorge Icaza presented a similar lament for a deceased woman, in which the widower moans, asking who will feed the guinea pigs, gather firewood, or check if the hen has laid an egg (Icaza 1964 [1934]:179). Quichua laments emphasize the loss of the loved one by focusing on the everyday activities of the deceased, according to traditional gender roles.

The moment when the family throws dirt on the coffin, to the ritual wailing of the women, is emotionally charged. Those who had been silent now openly express their grief, and from that point on the mood is somber.

FIGURE 5.2. Espirita Masaquiza spinning wool with her granddaughter Emilin.

The attendants return home, many having drunk wine and cane alcohol in their grief.

When Luis's twenty-three-year-old son died from lung disease, the young man's older sister told me sadly, "My brother was such a good uncle. He would help my sons with their homework, and he played soccer with them. He was really good to his nephews." Just outside the gate of the

cemetery, when the pallbearers rested the coffin at the gate before entering, the two teenaged nephews were overcome with grief. Their father,
Juan Manuel, stood hugging them both at once, trying to console them.
It was as if they couldn't move. One nephew was so overwhelmed that he
had trouble breathing and almost passed out. Friends ran to the vendors
to try to get him something to drink. It was a difficult and enormously
stressful time for Juan Manuel. He cared a lot for his wife's family, his wife
and sons were going through the shock and grief of this untimely death,
and he had spent the previous day with his in-laws at the hospital in the
city of Ambato. Since he is literate and speaks Spanish well, he translated
for his in-laws and fought with hospital administrators to get them to
release the body without charging more money.

I include this painful excerpt from my field notes because anthropological analyses of mortuary ritual and symbolism run the risk of portraying
death as devoid of emotion, loss, and pain in a way that objectifies the
mourners (Rosaldo 1989). The widow quietly sobbing alone on her porch
and the young adult nephews crying outside the gate of the cemetery
are examples of the spontaneous expressions of grief that occur outside
the ritualized actions of mourners (see Kan 1989:16–20). After the burial,
mourners express their affection for the deceased and commitment to
remember their loved ones through commemorative rituals.

Sending the Soul

The day after the burial the participants perform the Mondongo Misa at
the home of the deceased, in order to send the soul of the deceased off to
God. The Mondongo Misa is a ritual drama full of humor, yet it fulfills a
necessary ritual function. Two indigenous men dress up as Catholic priests
and are charged with sending the soul out of the space of the house and off
to heaven, called *jahua pacha* (the upper world) or *diusbuq llacta* (God's
land). In fact, Luis said that indigenous men perform the Mondongo Misa
because the Catholic priest doesn't come to the home of the deceased
for this ritual; therefore, indigenous men must dress up like priests and
perform the ritual themselves. While other Andean cultures enact humorous parodies of priests during important rituals (see Isbell 1985:144), the
appropriation of priestly powers here is necessary for the ritual transition of

sending the soul to God. It exemplifies a colonized people's appropriation of the powers of the colonizer through ritual mimesis (Taussig 1993).

Family, friends, and neighbors meet at the home of the deceased on the day of the Mondongo Misa. The family serves them food and cane alcohol. After eating and much drinking, two men dress as priests. Again, the daughters-in-law and other women related to the deceased through marriage (cachunguna) lend their long belts (chumbis) for the dramatic performance. After the ritual, the cachunguna have to "pay" with a liter of trago to get their belts back. The men wrap the belts around their ponchos to give the appearance of a priest's robe, and they put cloth or paper resembling a bishop's hat on their heads. There is some improvisation in each performance, but the general procedure is the same. The two priests sit on opposite sides of the patio. The priest closest to the door of the house is the *jahua uma*, meaning "upper head." The priest across from the house is the *ura chaqui*, "lower foot." Thus the division of space in the patio is a rare instance in Salasaca of the upper/lower duality that is common in other Andean cultures. Sometimes the mock priests get a notebook and pretend to be reading from the scriptures (Wogan 2004). They sprinkle maize beer on the guests in place of holy water and give out raw potato slices as the Catholic Eucharist. Then each priest leads a procession out of the patio to the back of the house and walks some distance away. The upper head priest goes to one place and the lower foot priest to another part. At one Mondongo Misa a man bent down and drew in the dirt, saying, "May the soul leave this earth." I later asked a neighbor what the man drew in the dirt, and he replied the man drew a circle, representing the devil's cauldron, and a line passing it, saying, "If you are good you will pass by the *paila* [devil's cauldron] and go right to heaven." At another Mondongo Misa, the "priest" drew in the dirt an image of Jesus with his crown of thorns. This part of the ritual varies depending on the performers.

Finally, the two "priests" pray to God to send off the soul. At this point others who are present will beg one "priest" to pray for their deceased relatives as well. Through this parody of priests the death of an individual is linked to the deaths of others, as people remember their own deceased family members. The prayer involves code-switching between Quichua and Spanish and is composed of Quichua orations interspersed with lines from the Catholic prayers Our Father and Hail Mary.

Luis explained the ritual transformation of sending the soul out of the space of the house and off to the upper world like this: "They ask with a prayer that the soul may go to the other life in a dream. The soul then goes from the house, leaving to go up. We say farewell. That's the way our ancestors would do it. That means that the soul doesn't come back." When I asked Luis why I had seen the mock priest draw in the dirt during one Mondongo Misa, he said "the 'priest' does so saying, 'May [the soul] leave Mother Earth' [*Ashpa Mama lluqshin nisha*]. Saying so that the dead doesn't stay in Mother Earth. The deceased leaves, and the living [*sano genteguna*] are left on earth."

According to Salasacans the Mondongo Misa "means that the soul never returns." But still another ritual is necessary to ensure that the personal belongings of the deceased are rid of his or her spirit. This ritual is called the *ucu pichana*, "cleansing of the inner room."

Cleansing the House: Ucu Pichana

Ucu pichana means "sweeping inside"; it involves sweeping the entire home of the deceased with medicinal plants and a guinea pig, the same materials used to cleanse the body of a person who is ill. It is the duty of the pallbearers to perform this ritual on the third day after the burial. During the ucu pichana the space inside the house must be cleansed of any remnants of the soul of the deceased. The dirt, straw from the bed, tattered clothing, and other remains from the room of the deceased are swept up, taken to a nearby crossroads, and burned along with the cleansing materials. "This means that the deceased is gone, even his trash" a pallbearer once explained to me.

Burning the refuse at a crossroads means the roads carry the substance, or essence, of the deceased away. Luis explained it like this: "On the last day they clean the inside, the home of the deceased, and throw everything in a crossroads . . . so that the soul may go in the wind, that the water may carry it." This process of throwing used medicinal plants into a crossroads so that the essence will be carried by the roads, the wind, and finally the river is also used with medicinal plants from a ritual cleansing of animal or human bodies to remove illness. This has to do with the concept of sami, or life essence (described in chap. 4). Luis explained why crossroads are central to the efficacy of the cleansing ritual:

In crossroads young people pass, adult people pass, elderly people pass, some of them have good thoughts [*alli yuyi charish gentega*], people with good sami. So that sami hits them. That sami goes; having hit them, the sami is carried by the wind, and the wind takes it to the river. In the river, the water gets it. When the water gets it, it goes carrying those bad things away. Then that bad stuff has left, then the weak body becomes strong as if an injection were given, as if oral medication were given. Now the bad has been taken out. That miracle is done from the crossroads to the water. Some animals, too, some that carry heavy loads, have tired samis. They get contaminated. Because at the crossroads, a road comes from this side, a road comes from that side, the people cross . . . all kinds of people, all kinds of samis. Young samis, adult samis, old samis, old women, old men, little children, all kinds of people pass in the crossroads.

According to Luis' explanation, then, it is the essence, or air, of people going in different directions that carries the *malguna*, the bad things that were cleansed out of the body, to the wind and then to the river to be carried away.

What I want to emphasize here is the significance of roads in Salasacan views of the landscape and the way by which these views structure rituals. In both healing rituals and the ucu pichana, roads carry away what has been cleansed. In healing rituals the intersecting roads carry away the sickness, and in the post-mortuary house-cleansing ritual, the roads carry away any residue of the soul of the deceased. In both cases, the wind takes the cleansed essences to the river, and in this way the body or house and the Salasacan landscape are all rid of negative essences.

The Incas practiced an analogous ritual: they would throw the remains of sacrificial offerings into the confluence of rivers (Burger 1992), called a *tinkuy*. The tinkuy represents the mediation of opposing forces. Similarly, the remains of Salasacan ritual and house cleansings are thrown into the juncture of roads so that the negative essences can be carried to the river and carried away. Although Salasacans do not use the word *tinkuy*, discourse and practice suggest a similar notion that the point of convergence is powerful.[2]

The Salasacan practices of huayru and the ucu pichana have precedents in the practices of early colonial Andean ancestor cults, which observed certain rites during the five days after death: "At the end of the five days, the dead person's close kin swept the home, removed belongings of the deceased in a bundle, and took them away to a ravine. The disposal of the belongings lifted the obligation to grieve publicly. The end of this period was, and still is, associated with ritual gambling using a die-like marked bone" (Salomon 1995:330). In addition to the continuation (in some form) of these ancient practices, Salasacans also use the Catholic feast day of the Body of Christ to perform commemorative rituals for the deceased.

Death, Ritual, and Memory

Social groups sustain collective memory through the performance of rituals (Connerton 1989). Peter Wogan (2004) has described how Salasacans use church literacy practices to commemorate their own ancestors during the Day of the Dead, observed on November 2. For this day, Salasacans take out a "list of souls," pieces of paper with the names of their deceased relatives. Salasacan families take the lists from their homes to the Catholic church for mass, where the priests read off the names and sprinkle holy water on the lists, thereby cooling off the souls. The lists represent the souls, which are said to be present during the Day of the Dead. Storing the lists in their homes allows Salasacan families to appropriate church powers. Salasacans repeatedly told Wogan that they keep the lists "to remember" their deceased relatives, but in fact, new lists are made up from memory each year. Wogan noticed that older, illiterate Salasacans had the names in their heads and dictated those names to literate people who made up new lists (rather than copying them from the old). Remembering, for Salasacans, means properly honoring the dead by performing the act of making the list. This memory act is repeated every year (Wogan 2004:98–104).

We can see the significance of ritual as a form of remembering when Salasacan families re-enact death rites during the Catholic feast-day celebrations of Corpus Christi in June. The way in which Salasacans use this feast day to commemorate their own family members shows how indigenous people shaped ritual to serve as a form of collective memory. Families may choose to have a mass, re-enact the rites that were performed at the funeral, and visit the cemetery during this celebration. If the purpose of the Mondongo Misa is to send the soul away from Mother Earth and off to heaven, why would it be necessary to perform the ritual again?

FIGURE 5.3. A commemorative mass in the cemetery. The "grandmother" volcano Tungurahua appears in the background.

Salasacans say they re-enact the death rites in order "to remember" the person. During the Corpus Christi celebrations, families that choose to commemorate a deceased loved one attend mass in the Catholic church. Then they follow the same road they took to the cemetery when they buried the deceased, stopping at crossroads to distribute wine. They perform the Mondongo Misa and prepare cachun api again. This is what Paul Connerton (1989:69) calls gestural repetition, the mimetic re-enactment of an earlier performance. In Salasaca, some families perform the commemorative rites as long as twenty years after the original funeral. At the cemetery, family members pour cane alcohol on the grave while saying a short prayer or talking to the deceased, and they ask an elder to say a blessing over the grave (fig. 5.3). Respect for elders is a strong value in Salasaca, so the older the man the better for bestowing the blessing. Luis has often been called upon to bestow such blessings in the cemetery. He gave me an example of the prayer he would give over a grave, using his father's grave as an example:

> [In Spanish] Our Father who art in heaven, hallowed be thy name. Thy kingdom come, thy will be done, on earth as it is in heaven.

[Switches to Quichua] You are the soul I send Father, Father, my dear little Father, you have now gone to the other life [*shug vidamumi ringui*], may God take care of you. You, Father, are before God, you are in the confession [*confesionbimigangui*] of yaya Dios [Father God]. You, before God, for all your sins that you have done, yaya Dios will judge you in the other world; you and your life will be praised and your life, as it has always been in this life. We haven't obeyed God, and to the Virgin Mary, Mother of God, we haven't believed in her [in the past]. For this reason we haven't lived by the right path but now, now that you are before God with the Virgin Mary and before Mama Virgen Mary, and now from this world you are already in the other world and now forever with the *angelitos* [deceased children] that were lost. The child angels also are in the other world, and now you are going to find each other [*tupanacunguimi*], the children angels with your mother, with your grandparents. And you are before the great God, you stand before yaya Dios and before the Mama Virgen, and before them and with all those who died, as they are living, you are in the other world, now that you have gone from this world you don't exist, and we have remained. But we also are going to follow other days or other years, only yaya Dios knows when will be the day that he takes us. Until then we are going to be wandering, so take care of us, now that you are in the other world before Tayta Dios, take care of all [whom] you are seeing that they be blessed, the blessing of the Father, the Son, and the Holy Spirit; three persons, one pumpkin God. And now we say good-bye, now that you go from here that's why we and all the family members and all the cousins and neighbors, we have all said to God, and to you, and now we say good-bye to you. We have remained in the name of God, of the Holy Spirit, in the name of yaya Dios in the name of the Father, the Son, and the Holy Spirit; three persons, one pumpkin God, may you be forgiven and may you take care of us well, Good-bye, good-bye, now we are going home.

The prayer starts out in Spanish with a portion of the Catholic Our Father, then switches to Quichua to express a variety of religious concepts from Catholic teachings and native Andean religious beliefs. Luis mentions a past lack of faith in God and in the Virgin Mary, and that "we haven't lived by the right path." This is the same analogy used by the

Salasacans in 1914, when they tried to convince church authorities to appoint a particular festival sponsor. The metaphor of "choosing the right path" to describe the practice of Catholicism by indigenous people has been incorporated into indigenous discourse: once as a persuasive tool in the letter to the archbishop (chap. 3), and now as part of the memorized oral text of a prayer said during commemorative death rites.

Intertextuality in Ritual Performance

As mentioned previously, a common aspect of ritual performance in Salasaca is intertextuality: the embedding of one type of performance in another. In chapter 4 I described the observation of funeral rites for a bread baby during the fiesta of Caporales. Mortuary rituals especially reference other ritual performances. The boys' mock performances at wakes imitate adult rituals during fiestas. This performance-within-performance also involves intertextuality, in that the boy playing the role of loa should properly recite the speech used in the presentation of the sponsors in the real Capitán fiesta. The funeral of an unmarried young adult incorporates a wedding performance in which a hen or rooster substitutes for the would-be spouse. After burial, the Mondongo Misa references the Catholic mass by imitating the performance of mass while substituting indigenous ritual items for Christian symbols. The June feast day of Corpus Christi includes the re-enactment of death rites by families.

Intertextuality in Salasacan ritual connects different social events to one another. Marriage and death, both rites of passage, embed and are embedded in celebrations of the feast days of the Catholic calendar. By indexing one another, these events express the holistic nature of Salasacan social life, of all the gatherings that bring people together in celebration, mourning, gaming, transitional passages, and play. They are expressions of Salasacan collective identity.

Scholars of ritual point to the important functions of repetition, or restored behavior (Schechner 2002), as a feature of ritual. Connerton (1989) demonstrates the role of ritual in sustaining collective memory. Barbara Myerhoff (1990) notes that because rituals are repetitions of many past performances, they provide a sense of comfort and continuity to distressed mourners at a time of death. Margaret Drewal, drawing on Schechner's work on performance, notes the two "modes of repetition" in rituals:

one is repetition within a particular ritual, such as a steady repetition of drumming or chanting. In Salasaca this occurs in ritual prayers, when the rezachic repeats lines such as "yaya Dios" to create a poetic rhythm. The other mode is the repetition of entire rituals, such as the annual fiestas: "Performers recover through memory (of myth, of rehearsal, of the last performance) organized sequences that they then re-behave. Thus a performance is based in actuality on an earlier performance. In this sense, performance is by its very nature intertextual by virtue of the embodied practices of the performers" (Drewal 1992: 3).

The Salasacan rituals are intertextual in that they include imitations of performances within performances, including parody. Drewal discusses parody in the sense of repetition with critical difference "paradoxically indicating both cultural continuity and change, authority and transgression, involving both creator and partaker in a participatory hermeneutics" (1992: 3–4). Take the example of the Mondongo Misa as a parody: the performers take care to imitate the clothing, ritual gestures, and symbolic objects used by Catholic priests during the performance of the mass. Yet, it is the critical difference that makes this a uniquely indigenous ritual: it is performed by indigenous men, in Quichua, using homespun woolen clothes, raw potato slices, and maize beer (see Wogan 2004). The performers gain dominant powers through mimesis, while simultaneously expressing alterity (Taussig 1993). Despite the humor in the parody, the performers are enacting a sacred ritual transformation of sending the soul to heaven. At wakes boys contribute to religious ritual in their own right by taking care to accurately imitate the ritual props and speech of fiesta performers.

Conclusion

In this chapter I discussed the performance of funeral rites and the special roles of blood relatives and affinal relatives in them. Special symbols communicate messages about the context in which they are used: mourning hats identify blood relations of the deceased; the changing names of foods indicate the context in which they are used: cachun api instead of puka api; huayru uchu instead of uchu; "blood" instead of sugarcane alcohol. Although people consume the same foods on other ritual occasions, they use these terms only in the context of funerals.

Mimesis and parody and games of chance serve important religious functions. Playing games serves as a way for the living to please the soul. Performing a marriage ceremony restores the Andean value of a complementary, gendered pair when there is an untimely death of a young adult. Through parodying priests, indigenous men appropriate the powers of ritual transformation. During Corpus Christi, people re-enact entire rituals as a way to remember deceased family members, thereby modifying the Catholic rite to serve as a means of sustaining genealogical memory. By performing the funeral rites again, people remember through ritual repetition.

Sergei Kan (1989:15) writes that "death forces human beings to confront the central questions of their existence—the relationship between the temporary and the permanent in social life, between the individual and the group, between the past and the present." Death disrupts human social relations, but rituals, including games, provide a course of action for the living, and even a way to entertain the recently deceased. As Kan explains, "To maintain the reality of this socially constructed world in the face of death, mankind often relies on religion or other powerful ideological systems that promise what Lifton (1983) calls a sense of 'symbolic immortality'— a continuous symbolic relationship between our finite individual lives and what has gone before us and what will come after" (Kan 1989:15).

The children's re-enactment of community fiestas during the wake, the playing of ritual games, the naming of previously deceased family members in prayers of the Mondongo Misa, the use of red porridge that links the death of an individual to the collective remembrance of the deceased in November, and the re-enactment of death rituals during fiestas as a way to remember the deceased, all these create the symbolic link between the biological death of an individual and the continued collective life of the community.

The history of Catholic indoctrination led to the transculturation of death rituals, as indigenous people re-centered Catholic symbols, rituals, and texts within indigenous frameworks. I now move on to part 2 of the book, turning from collective, commemorative rituals to the experience of individuals. In what follows I show how cultural patterns impinge on private consciousness, and how individual acts sustain a relationship with the sacred through shamanic sessions and mountain offerings.

PART II

Individual Acts and Personal Narratives

CHAPTER 6

Tales of Amazonia

Personal Narratives of Healing by Yumbos

SALASACA, JULY 4, 2002, 10:30 A.M. RADIO BROADCAST. The announcer this morning informed people that in the city of Riobamba were two shamans from the Amazonian Napo Province: "two shamans [*chamanes*] from the Association of Shamans of Napo Province will be attending to people. They are M. Shuango and Juan Vargas, cousin of the presidential candidate Antonio Vargas." The announcer then interviewed Juan Vargas, and emphasized again that the shamans were from Napo Province. In answer to one of the interview questions, Juan Vargas said, "I learned to heal from my grandfather when I was thirteen years old." He went on to announce that he and his colleague would be at a community center in Riobamba to treat people starting on Saturday and continuing for fifteen days, from 8 a.m. until 9 p.m., and then that the two resident medical doctors would also be approved to attend to people in the community.

Mariano and Anita listened to the same radio station every morning because the announcer would state the time every five minutes. This was a necessary tool for getting the kids off to school on time in a house that lacked clocks. The station also broadcast regional news, such as the announcement just quoted. The radio announcement alerting highlanders that they could take advantage of the presence of two Amazonian shamans who were visiting the Andes continued a long tradition of Andean desire for Amazonian spiritual powers. Although there are shamans throughout Ecuador, those from certain regions are believed to be especially powerful. In fact, the radio announcer stated that one of the shamans was the cousin of then presidential candidate Antonio Vargas, whose grandfather was known as a very powerful shaman from Puyo in Pastaza Province (D. S. Whitten 2003:259). In this chapter I analyze personal testimonies of people who were healed by lowland shamans to show how they perpetuate an old Andean tradition that attributes spiritual powers to Amazonian and other lowland shamans. This is the first of three chapters that show how cultural and historical patterns (in this case, a shamanic regional network) are lived out by individuals.

Modern Landscapes, Ancient Knowledge

One view of the people from the Amazonian tropical forest is that they possess ancient knowledge that has been lost by modern Andeans. According to a Salasacan man named Raúl, the elders used to tell him old tales about the Incas. He told me that the Incas had a network of underground tunnels connecting the mountains of the Andes, and that they were powerful, sorcerer-like beings who could "go to the moon, only with their thoughts." In discussing modernday sorcery, Raúl compared the yumbos, here meaning indigenous Canelos people of Pastaza Province, to the ancient shamans: "Those who ensorcel go to the Canelos, the back/ east region [*huashaorienteladomu*]. They ensorcel by cleansing with a candle. When they die, their souls, they say, also die. The old shamans were really fierce. [They were] yumbos. They're indigenous people. They speak like us but with a different tone." In comparing the Incas to powerful sorcerers, and the fierce shamans of olden times to modernday yumbos, Raúl expresses the idea that the modern people of the tropical forest have retained a lost art.

When plowing fields, people occasionally find material manifestations of past civilizations, such as ancient sherds, bones, and other objects. An old folk tale tells of how the Incas burrowed underground to avoid being baptized by the Spanish, and of how they took their treasures with them. Occasionally, these treasures reveal themselves to individuals through dreams. An individual who dreams of treasures or of fire burning in a particular place should get up in the middle of the night and go to that spot to start digging. Dreams, according to Raymond Firth (1973), link private and public symbolism. In dreams that reveal Inca treasure in specific locations, historical and cultural images impinge on private consciousness and find expression in the experience of dreams. A few people told me they had had such dreams but were too afraid to undertake the search for Inca treasure alone, in the middle of the night. One night in the summer of 2005, some people came from the town of Guaranda looking for Mariano, an old Salasacan shaman. They said that they had visions of flames at a particular spot in their town, indicating buried treasure there, and they wanted the shaman to go with them to dig it up. Mariano didn't want to go alone and said he would wait for his compadre, an Amazonian yumbo shaman, to accompany him. Thus history, cosmology, and sacred geography converged as the residents of Guaranda sought to draw on the powers of modern shamans to find Inca treasure.

In Ecuador, where a white, Catholic elite constructed a racist, classist society that placed urban whites at the top of the hierarchy and black and indigenous peoples at the bottom, multiple concepts of the landscape, ecology, race, power, and cosmology were mapped onto the human geography of the country. Frank Salomon describes the moral topography of Ecuador as a concentric space with Quito at the center and the outer forests as a refuge of ancient, aboriginal powers. In this view, the Amazonian tropical forest (or oriente region) is like a "reservoir" of ancient indigenous power and esoteric knowledge that stands opposed to the church and state power of Quito (Salomon 1981:195).

Indigenous peoples, marginalized from economic and state power, possess what anthropologists have identified as alternative powers (Adams 1975). Michael Taussig calls this the "power of the primitive." He states "it is not just that Indians and blacks have been identified with evil in the depths of a class structure mediated by whites ascending to the godhead, but that from those depths springs power" (Taussig 1987:168). In Colombia, indigenous healers from the Sibundoy Valley take advantage of colonial images of "Indian" occult powers, based partly on their knowledge of *yagé*, the hallucinogenic vine. "And for this they rely on the existence of shamans of the foothills or lowlands, not just for yagé, which only grows below the valley, but for the allegedly superior power of the shamans otherwise beneath them, literally and figuratively" (Taussig 1987:153). Similarly, for highland indigenous peoples Amazonian indigenous peoples possess superior knowledge and power of spiritual forces. Among Salasacans, the pejorative term *yumbo* is synonymous with "strong shaman."

Some older Salasacan men spent some time in their youth in Amazonian regions, working or serving in the army. An old Salasacan story tells of an ill-fated romance between a yumba woman and her Salasacan lover. According to the story, a young Salasacan man went to the oriente region and became engaged to a woman there. The woman and her parents were diviners, "people who know things that we Salasacans don't know." The woman hid the man in her house, under a juice strainer, so that her parents would not find him. But her parents smelled him and said, "Something smells raw here." Upon discovering him and learning that he was engaged to their daughter, they appeared to accept him. They called him "son-in-law" and everyone drank together in celebration. They all planned to go to the highlands, to Pelileo, to slaughter a pig for the wedding. They put the son-in-law to work in the forest, but he was there all day without cutting down a single tree. Upon seeing this, the yumba girlfriend said "my parents will kill him." In order that the yumbo parents would see him working (because they are diviners), she took a white handkerchief and folded it with needles, and blowing on it, she made water appear in an irrigation ditch. The young man had immediately to start to channel the water.

But something was wrong. The parents told the young man to start boiling water because they were going to slaughter a pig, but the young woman said that they were going to kill him rather than a pig. So she caused them to transform into something else so that the parents wouldn't find them. She became a fruit tree, and the man, in a different form, was picking fruit from the tree when the yumba mother came walking along the path. She asked the man, not recognizing him, if he had seen the couple and he said no. When she returned home her husband told her "that was him!" The mother said, "I'm going to get him," but the young woman made them change form again; this time they took the form of a cowboy with cattle. Again, the mother asked about the couple, not recognizing them, and when she returned home her husband again said "that was him." The couple changed form again, and the yumba girlfriend made clouds, wind, and rain, and her mother got lost on the path, which was full of thorns the mother couldn't pass through.

Now the couple came to Salasaca. The yumba girlfriend brought the man there so that her parents couldn't kill him, because they didn't want her to marry an outsider. But upon coming to Salasaca, the man did her wrong. He remembered the love he had for a Salasacan woman, and he married that woman instead. The yumba girlfriend went home crying, without getting married. But she said, "At twelve noon on the day of your wedding I will come in the form of a dove. The minute that you sit down to eat at the wedding, I'm going to send two doves." The groom didn't believe her. In revenge the woman sent two doves along the road. The doves arrived and landed on the table at the wedding feast. The female dove was the yumba, the male was (represented) the groom. The female dove began to speak and told everything—how the couple had changed form several times, and everything they had been through together. Then she said, "I won out over everything" and she fell to the ground. The two doves died, and so did the bride and groom. The people at the wedding picked up the doves and saw that they were empty inside, but stuffed with cotton. They said "this is sorcery."

This story shows Andean perceptions of Amazonian divinatory powers and the power of transformation. In telling this story Salasacans use the expression "one who blows has come," which I translate as "sorcery," because blowing on something is a way either to heal or to curse people. The shaman's breath contains part of his life essence, and powerful shamans blow on things and people to enact spiritual transformations. The theme of the wronged lover killing a couple on their wedding day is understood by Salasacans. Before Salasaca had its own church, couples would marry in the church in Pelileo. Upon walking back to Salasaca for the wedding celebrations, the couple would always pass by Cruz Pamba. An old tradition held that a jilted lover could wait on the hill above Cruz Pamba and sever a rope into two pieces just as the couple approached the crossroads. This, it was believed, could cause the death of either the bride or groom, preventing them from living out their marriage together. The old story I tell here presents a somewhat different version: the jilted yumba-lover-diviner enacts her revenge by coming in the form of a dove. The theme of women turning into doves appears in Quichua poetics in both the Andes and Amazonian regions. Michael Uzendoski (2005: 55–57) recorded a song by a Napo Runa woman who described turning herself into a dove to follow a husband who abandoned her, and he compares this song to an ancient story told in the Huarochirí Manuscript in which a mythical woman turns into a dove to escape from a lover. Since pre-Columbian times, people have used the image of the dove to represent a lover in songs and poetry (Saroli 2005:50). The story of the yumba lover is rich with the imagery of Quechua love songs and poems and has precedents in pre-Columbian Quechua traditions. Andean love poetry often focuses on the loss of one's beloved through either abandonment or death.

Personal Narratives

Salasacans have long had direct experience with Amazonian spirituality, and personal testimonies of being healed by yumbos represent one aspect of Andean-Amazonian relations. Here I present two stories of Salasacans who were healed by yumbos. In the first narrative, an elderly woman tells how long ago, when she was a child, she was healed by a yumbo. In the second story, a man tells of how he was healed by an Amazonian shaman during one of the most significant events in Ecuador's history of indigenous struggle: the 1992 March for Land and Life in which indigenous peoples marched from Amazonia to the nation's capital and won land rights.

Before the construction of the modern roads that connect Ambato to Puyo, white merchants hired Salasacans to work as porters and walk to the Canelos region to sell products. Canelos people also traveled up through the highlands, selling tropical forest products, healing people, and providing the vision-producing brew called *ayahuasca*,[1] meaning "soul vine." One of these yumbos healed a woman named Rosa many years ago. I first learned of Rosa's experience in 1992 from her grandchildren, who told me that when their grandmother was young, she was healed by a yumbo who told her that she would live to be very old. Years later, in 1998, I asked Rosa about the experience and recorded her story in Quichua. At the time of the recording, Rosa's son estimated that she was in her mid-eighties. She recalled that she was very ill once as a child:

> My mother said [to the yumbo], "She's going to die." "She's not going to die," he said. "She's not going to die. She will live to be old. She will have a long life."
>
> An Otavalan [someone from the Andean town of Otavalo] was made to come first. The yumbo healed me after that, but the first one was an Otavalan. That Otavalan said, "I don't know, if she lives, she'll live, but if she doesn't live, she'll die. She'll die," he said to my mother. My mother cried. "I only have two little children" she said, because it was just my sister and me. For that reason my mother cried. "She's

going to die!" Saying that, in contrast, my mother got a yumbo from the oriente to cure me. He came here, he healed me here [in Salasaca]. That yumbo said, "She won't die, she will live to be very old." When that yumbo healed me, my mother was happy. . . .

The yumbos used to just pass through here. Those dear yumbos of the past used to carry calabash bowls like this, they would carry baskets on their heads, going down that road. They spoke *runa shimi* [Quichua] and they were from the east, from Canelos. They would pass through here carrying chambira fibers, calabash bowls, and ointments. My mother called on one to heal me. She was buying *calabash bowls*, she was buying *ointments*, and *I was also* healed. After that yumbo healed me I didn't get sick. He told my mother that she should give me cat and dog testicles to eat. He healed with plants and by sucking [to extract the illness from the body]. That yumbo said, "She won't die. She'll have a long life," he said.

At this point, Rosa's son added, "She even survived getting hit by a car." Indeed, Rosa lived to be very old. Although her exact age was not known, she passed away about a year after her great-great-grandchild was born.

This narrative tells of a yumbo from the Canelos people of the Amazonian tropical forest who was able to heal Rosa after at least one highland shaman failed. In addition to the repetition that is characteristic of Quechua poetics ("she won't die, she's not going to die"), Rosa's intonation emphasized certain words to create a parallel structure between the products sold and services rendered by the shaman. She similarly emphasized the *pilche* (calabash bowls), *pumada* (ointments), and *ñucatash* (I also), to create the sense that superior healing powers are one more exotic product brought by the yumbos to the highlands. The vertical exchange of lowland goods and magical services for payment from highlanders continues colonial practices in which Andeans contracted the services of lowland shamans and sorcerers (Salomon 1983:422). The structure of the narrative, in which the supernaturally superior yumbo saved Rosa when all hope seemed lost, can be compared to another Andean narrative recorded by Rudi Colloredo-Mansfeld. This narrative involved a "yumbo" not from the Amazonian region but from the western lowland region of Santo Domingo de los Colorados, which is famous for its powerful shamans. The narrator, Julio Toaquiza, told of years of personal and economic hardship:

> Despairing over years of fruitless effort and the physical toll it had taken, Julio visited a shaman who lived near Santo Domingo de los Colorados. "That lowland [*yumbo*] shaman [*chay yumboca*] told me, 'you will have work. Before you suffered. You will now have your own work. You will not have to go around suffering like you have.'" The shaman informed Julio that a dream [*muscui*] would reveal his work and that he must not let go of that dream. Soon, a dream inspired him to paint a drum for a fiesta. (Colloredo-Mansfeld 2003:279)

From there, Julio met a famous Quiteña art dealer who began to buy his work.

Both narratives use repetition when quoting the yumbo shamans, to emphasize the prescience of their predictions: Rosa quotes the yumbo as stating confidently that she would not die but would live a long life; Julio quotes the shaman as twice saying "you will have work." Both stories express a moral topography in Ecuador in which Andeans can tap into the spiritual powers possessed by lowland shamans.

Rosa's healing took place many years ago, when the yumbos would occasionally travel on foot through Salasaca. Amazonian shamans passed through Salasaca again in 1992, when they marched to Quito to demand protection of lands and indigenous rights. Several political organizations, including the Organization of Indigenous Peoples of Pastaza, came together to organize the march, and they were supported by highland and national indigenous organizations, the best known of which is CONAIE. Salasacans, like other highland indigenous peoples, were called upon to support their indigenous brothers by providing food and lodging during the long march, and representatives from every indigenous community were sent to Quito to show their support. The participants included Amazonian shamans, whose ayahuasca visions during the march assured the people of victory and gave them strength to go on. It is another example of indigenous peoples' use of multiple sources of power: the shamans, using the spiritual forces of the hallucinogenic tropical forest "soul-vine," provided the symbolic strength for people to continue and gain political power as manifested in the government's guarantee of titled land rights (D. S. Whitten 2003; N. Whitten, Whitten, and Chango 1997).

During the march, blanco-mestizos and highland indigenous people also took advantage of this source of Amazonian power. During their stop in Salasaca, some community members paid the shamans good money in order to be healed (N. Whitten, Whitten, and Chango 1997). A Salasacan man named "Carlos" told me how he approached a shaman to heal his blisters and chronic headaches while the Salasacan community was hosting the marchers:

> The healer said he was a Shuara.[2] I found him in the community center. He was one who came with the march; he stayed for a week, he didn't go to Quito. This healer only cured with plants; he boiled all the plants in water and told me to take off my clothes. "This is for the cold," he said; that's why I had those blisters. "Maybe we'll cure it," he said. After he cured me, I got better, and since that moment I have never had any blisters or anything again. And my headaches were relieved, too. I had been suffering from chronic headaches, and after this I got better. First, the doctors couldn't cure me. Rather, this healer healed me but afterwards he [divined] for me in a candle and he told me, "I'm going to tell whether someone has done harm to you" and there he told me "they have done you harm. You have had enemies also; they are envious, that's why they have done harm to you [i.e., to both Carlos and his wife], to your bodies, that's why you two haven't been able to have money, you can't move ahead," he told me, that's why he healed us. We told him to come back, but after leaving he never returned.

I asked Carlos who had done this to him, but he didn't want to say. "I can't tell you," he said. "If I tell you, they will come to investigate me and make problems for me." But he said he knew who this person was that caused them harm: "You also can see in a dream, drinking ayahuasca, but [the shaman] said, 'In another trip when I come I'm going to bring it' but he didn't come. But I wanted to see, by drinking ayahuasca, in order to see which one has done this to me. I thought about looking for him [when he didn't come back] but I don't know where he lives."

The spiritual powers attributed to shamans are believed to be used for healing but are also feared. There are narratives about ancient times, as well as occasional gossip about strange deaths, that implicate the yumbos of the oriente as the medium for carrying out a Salasacan's harmful desires. The script of such narratives usually refers to an angry individual who takes either clothing or dirt from the victim's footprint to the yumbos in order to ensorcel the victim.

For highland shamans, a relationship with or training by yumbos is symbolic capital (Bourdieu 1990). Shamans tell their clients how much time they spent in the Amazon region, or let them know that they "work with" yumbos on a spiritual-cooperative level. Highland shamans from the Otavalan region make regular trips to the Amazonian region to maintain their spiritual power (Butler 2006:128). The Association of Indigenous Shamans of Napo now has a formal training program, as I learned from the certificate of completion that a young, new healer from Salasaca proudly displayed on his wall in 1996. I explore this relationship more in the next chapter.

Perceptions of the moral topography of Ecuador are based in part on the history of highland-lowland connections, and this history includes exchanges of shamanic knowledge. Taussig (1987) traces the colonial constructions of Amazonian indigenous peoples as "primitive," "savage," and spiritually powerful. Lowland shamans may exploit such images in order to capitalize on the stereotypes, but Amazonian shamanism is part of a long tradition related to the larger cosmological system in which the shaman operates (N. Whitten 1976). This cosmological system includes ecological symbolism, forest and water spirits, mythology, and history and is expressed in visions, dreams, narratives, and ceramic arts (N. Whitten 1976; D. S. Whitten and Whitten 1988). Shamans heal not only outsiders, but also their own people.

The individual experiences of Salasacans who consult lowland shamans continue the tradition of highlanders contracting lowland shamans. As people tell their success stories, they perpetuate this moral topography of Ecuador, just as narratives about seeking out yumbos for sorcery maintains a view of Amazonia (and Santo Domingo to the west) as places with spiritually powerful inhabitants. The historical, cultural pattern of modern landscapes as retainers of ancient knowledge is maintained by individual actors. The next chapter focuses on Salasacan shamans, their appropriation of Amazonian spirituality, and their use of local sacred mountains.

CHAPTER 7

Shamanism

IN 1885 SALASACA WAS AN ANNEX of the parish of Pelileo. The archbishop's delegation would periodically make inspections, called *visitas*,
of parishes throughout Ecuador and record the state of affairs of each
parish, and the archbishop's recommendations for it, in the "Autos de
visitas pastorales." During the inspection of the parish of Pelileo in 1885,
the archbishop of Quito, José Ignacio Ordoñez, noted a problem with
"sorcerers" in the area: "The beliefs and superstitions of the brujos [witch
doctors] are a great obstacle to the faith; and as we have known that in
this parish there are some who claim themselves as such, they will be
persecuted without rest, until this town and its annexes are purged of such
a plague" (Autos de visitas pastorales, Pelileo, Nov. 6, 1885).

Since the early colonial days of evangelization, the existence of shamans (Sp. *brujos*; Qu. *jambij*), native priests, and diviners in Ecuador was
considered one of the major obstacles to Christianizing the indigenous
people. Priests publicly punished shamans and publicly burned their
ceremonial objects. Nevertheless, shamans continue to practice healing
rituals and divination to this day, and they are sought out by blanco-
mestizo as well as indigenous clients. Shamanism has remained one of the
most steadfast indigenous religious practices, and a study of shamanism is
necessary to any understanding of indigenous religion. This is not to say
that it has remained unchanged; rather, shamanism is a form of native
South American religious practice that people have adapted to historical transformations. For example, political turmoil, interethnic conflict,
power struggles for positions in the colonial system, and land disputes in
the eighteenth-century Audiencia de Quito led to increased power for
some shamans and persecution for others. Shamans also increased their
prominence by convincing others of their access to various sources of
power, including knowledge of Hispanic and Afro-Ecuadorian cultural
systems (Salomon 1983).

Salasacan shamans draw on the powers of the famous "Colorado"
shamans of Santo Domingo to the northwest, Amazonian shamans of

the oriente, and mountain spirits. This moral topography of Ecuador probably has roots in pre-Columbian trans-regional trade networks. Frank Salomon (1986:109) cites a 1610 report of Tsátchela (known as "Colorado Indian") traders traveling from the western lowlands, up through Ambato (near Salasaca), to the Amazonian region. The report indicates that they were exchanging ceremonial objects for certain herbs, suggesting that the pre-Columbian exchanges east and west of the Andes involved objects of ceremonial as well as utilitarian importance and may have involved the exchange of shamanic knowledge. Recall from chapter 6 that Rosa included the yumbo shaman's healing powers in a list of lowland products that could be obtained from yumbos passing through the highlands. This trans-regional network of shamanic knowledge continues today and figures prominently in indigenous artistic depictions of shamanism from Tigua (D. S. Whitten 2003).

Salasacan shamans serve as mediators between cultural knowledge and individual experiences of illness and healing. Socially and ritually, they fulfill a role as mediators between the human body, the soul, and the landscape. This chapter, and the next, show Andean practices of mountain veneration and healing during the time of my fieldwork (1990–2008), and the relationship in Salasacan cosmology among the landscape, illness, and healing. The common local topographic features that shamans use (shown in fig. 1.3) include the two connected mountains Quinchi Urcu and Palama, which stand above the Cruz Pamba crossroads to form a complex of sacred sites. Some also use the mountain Teligote and local sacred springs.

Shamans serve as mediators between the sacred landscape and individual bodies in several ways. First, Shamans gain the power to heal from a sacred place, sometimes by sleeping in that place. Second, shamans interpret physical ailments as caused by a connection between the human body and a place, and healing often involves recovering part of a person's soul from a mountain or other topographic feature. Third, shamans call upon the spirits of Ecuadorian mountains to "collaborate" with them during the healing rituals. Finally, as I explained in chapter 6, the human geography of Ecuador, as constructed by Salasacans and others, plays a significant role in healing rituals. Shamans in Salasaca call on the spirits of healers from lowland ecological zones to help them heal their patients.

Illness and Mountain Offerings

Unborn children, like sleeping people, are in a state of liminality which leaves them vulnerable to the landscape. A place can steal part of a child's soul and this appears as a birthmark or loss of part of the body when the child is born. The event is traced back to a time when the pregnant mother fell asleep near a mountain. It seems that not only is the child in the womb vulnerable to the landscape, but when the mother is in a state of sleep, the child is in particular danger of losing its soul, and therefore part of its body, to a mountain. A woman explained that her twelve-year-old daughter's shortened earlobe was something that happened when she was pregnant with the girl. She and her husband went to Otavalo (about a five-hour bus trip) to visit her husband's godfather, an indigenous Otavalan. He lived near the foot of a mountain there. They spent the night in the godfather's house, at the foot of the mountain. The mother explained that the mountain "caught" (*urcu japin*) and "took" part of the unborn child's ear. The child's grandfather explained: "The ear, the hand, or anything, it comes out damaged. Fortunately, it only took that, just a little. If not, [the mountain would have taken] everything. If the whole mountain had taken it, it would have taken the whole ear."

Another woman, Juana, told me about her niece, whose eye is discolored with a dark spot:

> They say the mountain took it. A mountain from that side, called Cungu Urcu. There, [the mother] slept when she was pregnant. The mother went to work on a minga to get potable water. She went to go rest during the lunch hour. After eating, she closed her eyes and fell asleep. The mountain took that child; the eye is totally black. The mother left guinea pigs, she left them dressed with all colors [ribbons], she sent them as payment [to the mountain] saying, "Send my child." She paid everything to the mountain. She left twelve guinea pigs to that mountain. But the eye is still dark.

Juana did not know why the mountain would want to "take" part of a child, but said it can happen to unborn children if a pregnant woman sleeps near any mountain. Of course, leaving offerings to the mountain does not always work; but people reported successful cases as well as unsuccessful ones like the case just mentioned.

Birthmarks are explained as the result of the baby being "kicked" by the mountain (*urcu jaitushca*) while in the mother's womb, and shamans offer this explanation not only for local women, but also for blanca-mestiza mothers who take their babies to be cured by Salasacan shamans.

Children are susceptible to environmental illnesses. These include illnesses caused by soul-stealing mountains (*urcu apan*), being "persecuted" by the rainbow (*cuichi catin*), sleeping in abandoned places, which can cause a child to go mad, sleeping near pigs or in a place where pigs have slept, being persecuted by unknown spirits (*diablo catin*), and fright sickness, called *espanto*. Cures for these illnesses include leaving offerings to sacred places. In the case where a specific mountain is believed to have the child's soul, a payment, such as a guinea pig wrapped with colored threads, will be left to that mountain in order to restore the child's soul. If the child has espanto, which may be characterized by nightmares, excessive crying, or diarrhea, a shaman might do a ritual cleansing of the child and the house, in order to exorcise the house of any "devils." In general, anyone can do a medicinal cleansing (*pichana*) by sweeping plant bundles of *marco* (*Franseria artemisoides*), ruda (*Ruta graveolens*), *ortiga* (nettle, Qu. *tsini*), and *santamaría* (?), over the child and leaving the plants in a crossroads, in the middle of the highway, or at Cruz Pamba. People also take children to Cruz Pamba to have them roll around in the sacred dirt there. In order to increase the ritual efficacy, someone other than the parent should take the child. For many cures, including medical doctors' prescriptions, parents say the cure or ritual must be administered by *mano de otro*, that is, "the hand of an outsider," someone outside of the family. Also, when someone takes the child to Cruz Pamba, one road must be taken on the way there and a different one on the way back. After rolling in the dirt on the sacred ground, the child's clothes must be reversed, called *lluquishca* (*lluqui* is the Quichua word for "left" and "reversed"). These precautions signify a transformation in which after rolling in the sacred dirt, the previous condition is reversed.

Just as the unborn child in the womb is susceptible to soul loss while the mother sleeps, so the young child is susceptible to soul loss while asleep and in a dream state. "The mountain takes the child's soul in a dream" people told me. After this, the mountain does not allow the child to sleep; the mountain continues pulling the child's soul in a tug-of-war, expressed as *aisajichan* or *chutijichan*. The word *aisana* means "to take something by the hand," such as when one leads an animal to pasture by pulling it on a rope. The word *chutana* means "to pull." Adding the *-ji* (or *-qui*) infix implies a resistance to the pulling, a back-and-forth process in which one force is pulling one way and another force is pulling in the opposite direction or resisting the pulling force. The restless sleep of a child who has slept by a mountain is cited as evidence that the mountain is pulling the soul from the child, while the soul is resisting, trying to stay with the child.

A 1997 case of an illness tells us what happens when a child's soul is not restored. I went with Manuel, the shaman, to make a house call to perform a healing ritual for a young adult man who lived down by the river. The young man had been suffering from dizzy spells, and one day while working he almost passed out. Before starting the ritual, the shaman spoke to the mother of the patient and the two determined that the condition was the result of a long progression of an illness that began when the man was a child and fell asleep outside, during which time the mountain took his soul. Because he wasn't cured right away, the "ataque" went on maturing (*phukusha*) little by little, darkening his heart. The shaman would have to call on the mountain to return his soul, and if that didn't work, they would have to go there to leave an offering. A couple of weeks later the man's sister-in-law told me that the cure had worked and they had not needed to leave an offering.

Adults who visit a mountain for the first time or who sleep on a mountain also risk leaving their souls behind. When someone visits a mountain for the first time the mountain causes that person to dream (*soñachina*). The person must go a second time in order to recover his or her soul. When I went with a group of Salasacans to the mountain Teligote to gather medicinal plants, Manuel called his own name when we were leaving, saying, "Let's go Manuel, don't stay behind, I'm going now. My soul leaves a photograph behind [*ñuca alma foto saquirín*]. I'm going to my land of Salasaca." By stating that his soul leaves a photograph behind Manuel was using photography, an image replica, to express the idea that the soul leaves something of itself behind. However, the soul seems to have more than one manifestation, or it is capable of being multilocal.

Cultural definitions of illness include *ataques* (attacks), of which there are several different kinds. Ataques are based on where the person has been, especially while in the vulnerable sleep state. Sometimes the victim falls down a lot during the new or full moon "like a drunk person." The ataque is always there, but the body resists the effects until the new or full moon. An ataque results from sleeping in abandoned places, such as when a small child falls asleep in a dirt path, or when a drunk passes out in an abandoned place or near a dangerous place, or when someone rests near pigs or in the place where pigs have been resting. Different kinds of ataques have different symptoms. Children who fall asleep in open paths could go crazy. Some people can be cured of the ataque if the exact cause is known, for instance, if the ataque can be traced to a specific mountain or place. Others are never cured.

One man in the community was said to have gone mad and to suffer from delirious behavior during the new and full moon. The cause, according to neighbors, was that he and his family went to shamans to be "blown" (*phukuna*) for good luck; a ritual using the power of sami. According to hearsay, the whole family received luck and became rich after they were "blown on" by the shaman, but the one man went crazy. Power is a delicate weapon that can bring protection, luck, or serious alterations of one's mind.

The Healing Ritual

Prior to receiving shamanic services, the patient must be diagnosed through a guinea pig cleansing. This involves the shaman rubbing the live guinea pig over the patient's entire body. The guinea pig is choked to death during the process and then skinned, and the shaman examines all the internal organs for any little details. According to Salasacans the guinea pig reflects exactly what is in the patient's body, therefore female patients must use female guinea pigs, and male patients must use male guinea pigs, in order to accurately mirror the reproductive organs. The shaman shows the insides of the guinea pig to the patient and the patient's family and discusses the details with them. In one case the shaman showed the heart of a guinea pig used to cleanse a small boy. The heart was "cooked," indicating that the child was suffering from fright sickness due to a previous incident in which he had fallen off the back of a pickup truck.

After the diagnosis is made, the family of the patient makes an agreement with a shaman to return in order to begin the healing ritual. The ritual is most effective if performed on a Tuesday or Friday, and some-times the patient needs to be cleansed twice, once on Tuesday and again on Friday. The patient should bring cologne, a candle, and trago (cane alcohol) to the shaman's house. The shaman's *mesa*, his table of power objects, includes ancient objects such as axe- or T-shaped stones, black shiny stones, conch shells, and old coins. The general model of the ritual involves a cleansing of negative substances from the patient's body. This cleansing is accomplished through (1) rubbing, which transfers some of the impurities out of the body; (2) spraying with a mist of liquids, includ-ing trago, cologne, holy water, and detergent; and (3) fumigation with cigarette smoke and by smoking medicinal plant bundles. Eggs, candles, and special stones are used for the cleansing. Some shamans "read" the candle after the patient cleanses with it by lighting it and studying the flame. The plant bundles are used for both cleansing and fumigation, and the shaman blows alcohol through a flame to produce a flash of fire over the patient, which some shamans describe as mastery of lightning. Other techniques of protection are used, such as putting old coins, alcohol, and strong-smelling substances, including cinnamon, *ishpingo* (Amazonian cinnamon), and garlic, into a metal cup and burning them. The smells keep bad spirits away. Finally, the shaman sucks the illness out of the patient's head and chest and spits it out.

In order to give insight on the significance of geography and space in healing rituals, I focus here on the ritual of one particular shaman and compare it to the rituals of two other men. All three shamans I discuss here use techniques that have been observed in other shamanic cultures, including altered states of consciousness (Townsend 1997:432; Winkelman 1997:401), achieved through the consumption of cane alcohol; possession of a collection of power objects on a mesa (Calderón et al. 1999; Glass-Coffin 1998); mastery of spirits (by summoning mountain spirits and the spirits of other powerful shamans through chants); and extraction of illness by sucking it from the patient's body (Townsend 1997:451; Lévi-Strauss 1985 [1963]). In addition to these widespread techniques of shamanism, we can trace some aspects of Salasacan shamanism to pre-Columbian cosmologies in the North Andes. I have already mentioned the use of a guinea pig for diagnosis of illness, something which the colonial Arch-bishop Alonso de la Peña said could be tolerated, as long as it did not imply a pact with the devil. The archbishop advised that many substances have natural properties that can cure ailments, and since humans were ignorant of these natural properties, "cleansing" (by rubbing the sick person) with objects such as maize, chile peppers, and guinea pigs was allowable (Peña Montenegro 1995 [1668]:504). Likewise, the practices of leaving used medicinal plants in crossroads and of leaving offerings on mountaintops were classified as either idolatry with heresy, exterior idolatry, or vain observance, depending on whether the petitioner saw divinity in these places. Although the clergy saw shamans as an obstacle to evangelization, some healing practices were tolerated. The rituals of Salasacan shamans are comparable in many ways to shamanic rituals throughout South America. My focus here is on individual practice: the meanings of shamanic rituals to the specialists and the clients, and the way by which Salasacans maintain their religion through interactions with shamans.

Manuel

Manuel refers to the black stones and axe-shaped objects on his mesa as "weapons" (*armas*). After he cleanses the patient with the medicinal plant bundles, he blows sugarcane alcohol and cologne over the body and then over the plant bundles, which he sets on fire, then spits more alcohol through the flames to create a burst of light. He then sucks the sickness out of certain parts of the body, especially the heart (*shungu*), with his mouth. After rubbing the body with the stones he begins his chant. He explained:

> Then I call on those back-east yumbos [*huashalado yumboguna*]. The Otavalans [of Andean Imbabura Province], Chimborazo, Imbabura, Cotopaxi [mountains]. Making the call, first to begin: Imbabura, Cotopaxi, this Tungurahua, Yanaurcu, Chimborazo. From there, again, begins the back-east yumbos, Archidona, Napos, Pastaza [regions of the Amazon where powerful shamans live]. Some of them come in order to help. We call the shadows. From there, on the other hand, we call Santo Domingo Colorado [a lowland western province of the Tsáchela indigenous people]. Those indigenous people, the ones that are called, come to accompany us. The shadow comes, *sombra*. They cleanse the bodies; they fix them in order to make them better. In this

way, healing begins, only in *runa shimi* [Quichua]. From there, after finishing with the mesa, after that we sing. At this moment the one that is healing calls them. At the moment that we call them, they arrive. When we finish, the last thing we do is place the patient's clothes on the table and blow on them. From there then we call, we say Virgin of Lajas, Virgin of Quinche, Virgin of Paz, and then we finish.

Manuel calls on the "shadows" of distant mountains and healers from the Amazonian region as well as Santo Domingo de los Colorados. The Colorado indigenous people are self-named Tsáchela and are known throughout Ecuador as powerful shamans. Manuel draws on various geographical regions of Ecuador and on places where there are strong devotions to the Catholic Virgin Mary, in order to heal his patients.

I recorded Manuel's healing rituals on different occasions in 1991–1992. During the ritual, Manuel sings repeatedly the names of the mountains and the provinces of powerful shamans, hardly pausing between names: "Yumbos Saracay Archidona del oriente Napos Pastaza Tungurahua Llanganati Carihuairazo Cotopaxi Imbabura Santo Domingo de los Colorados Yumbo! [speeds up incantation, speaks in a rough, strained voice] Napos Pastaza Archidona del oriente Imbabura Tungurahua Llanganati Shuuun!" Figure 7.1 shows the relative locations of the mountains and places summoned by Manuel in his chant.

Manuel says that he "works with" the yumbos from the oriente, because their shadows come to "collaborate" with him in order to heal. Manuel is also ritual kin to a shaman from the Andean town of Otavalo. The Otavalan shaman is the godfather of Manuel's oldest son, José. Once, when the godfather was visiting, José and his family requested that the shaman perform a healing. José had been drinking a lot and was not working. Although José was a skilled mason, work in the region is physically hard but pays very little, and jobs are sporadic and temporary. His wife and parents were angry with him, and José recognized the problem. His Otavalan godfather did a "cleansing" so that José would stop drinking and look for work. After the cleansing, José announced that he was going to stop acting like a lazy drunk and look for work, and he did. As with any therapy, the person must admit the problem and want to change. The shamanic cleansing marks a transformation, giving the patient the confidence that he is now cured.

FIGURE 7.1.   Map of sacred places and mountains invoked for healing.
(Map by Jacqueline Fewkes)

Manuel has healed many Salasacans, including members of his own family, and his reputation extends far beyond Salasaca. On several occasions people have even come from other provinces to have Manuel heal them. Many are small-town blanco-mestizos, people who are considered slightly socially superior to indigenous people.[1] The fact that members of the dominant Hispanic, mestizo culture seek out the spiritual powers of people who are considered "marginal" and backward shows the attribution of superior supernatural powers to classes of people who lack economic, political, and social power. This "power of the primitive" is based on the same ideology that I discussed in chapter 6, in which those who live deep in the "uncivilized" Amazonian forest are considered to be superior shamans and bearers of ancient knowledge.

Pablo

Pablo is proud that he spent some time in the oriente learning about shamanism from the yumbos, even though Salasacan healing rituals are different from those of Amazonian shamans. Pablo's rituals vary slightly with each performance, and he intersperses the sessions with personal stories as he consumes more and more trago. During the ritual he names the places of Qishpichunga, Salamanga, Guaytacamac, Archidona, Tena, Pastaza, and the yumbos. He names his own hamlet in Salasaca. He says that he heals "with" Jesus and the Virgin of Huaycu, and he calls on mountain spirits. The use of the patient's sami is integral to the ritual; the patient breathes on the healing stones before being cleansed. Pablo yells "sombra!" (shadow) as he sweeps the medicinal plant bundles and old, black shiny stones over the patient. During one of his healing rituals, Pablo's young adult son walked into the room and hung a photograph of his recently estranged wife on the wall. "Blow well so that she comes back to me," he said, referring to the power of the shaman's sami. Manuel, Pablo, and Miguel, another shaman, create "lightning" by spitting sugarcane alcohol and cologne over a burning plant bundle. This creates a quick burst of flames over the patient, in most cases without burning the person.

Miguel

Miguel names each of the stones and axe heads on his mesa after the geographic location of its origin. He has Naríz de Diablo, a mountain in Tungurahua Province and also the name of an area on the railroad line to Santo Domingo de los Colorados; Guayaquil (the largest city in Ecuador, on the coast); Santo Domingo; Tungurahua; and the local, smaller mountains of Nitón and Quinchi Urcu. He says he found stones in these places because he has luck. But instead of referring to the stones as weapons, as Manuel does, he says that the stones *are* the mountains, and he "has" the mountains in the stones on his table. As he showed me his mesa, he explained:

> This is the mountain Sucabón in Santo Domingo. Carihuairazo, and the Oriente, Archidona, and Sangay. With these I pray. Look, this one has a foot [referring to a natural formation in the stone]. They are hard [he bangs the stones together, making a metallic sound]. One hundred mountains are arranged here. These are the Llanganates, so that I can cleanse the shungu [heart, central organ]. *It* cures, not me. They are mountains. If God helps me, I work with these. This is Quinchi Urcu [he shows me a ball-shaped stone]. This is [the local sacred spring] Galapago. This one is Curipugyu [a medicinal spring located near the border of Salasaca]. I used to go during the full moon and the new moon. Bathing there one never gets sick. I used to go to look for rocks. But now I have the rocks, and I don't go anymore. These are from beyond here, from Nitón Cruz. These are from Palama. This one has a heart, this one intestines. These are from here, from Punta Rumi [a dangerous rock]. These rocks are *educados* [domesticated, civilized, trained] now. If there is something bad, these rocks work. When I say it like this, it works. I read the Bible. I cleanse with these mountains, with the Santo Domingo stone, the Santo Domingo forest stone, Santo Domingo, Carihuairazo, Oriente Archidona Sangay, San Borondong, Naríz de Diablo, San Antonio de Guayaquil. With all sixty mountains I call, I can heal anything, with the mountains.

As I was interviewing Miguel one day in 1996, a blanco-mestizo man from the town of Pelileo came and interrupted us. The man demanded an immediate divination as to whether he should invest in a business with his friend. He clearly knew Miguel as a shaman and was relying on him to help make the decision: "My friend has this idea to invest in buses as a business, and he wants me to partner with him. I need to know whether this business will be successful, but he wants to know today. Hurry up! I need you to tell me now!" He wanted Miguel to "read" into a candle for him, a type of divination in which the shaman lights a candle and studies the flame.

For Miguel, certain stones, representing places, are good for healing particular parts of the body. Other Salasacans have associated local springs with healing powers for particular body parts. The comparison of rituals of three different shamans shows that Salasacan healers draw on different power sources during the rituals. These vary by individual but include the topographic features of the Ecuadorian landscape, Jesus Christ, and the Catholic Virgin Mary in her various manifestations in specific places. For example, Manuel prays to Father Sun and Father Moon (Inti Tayticu, Luna Tayticu) when he leaves a mountain offering, and then prays to the virgins who are patrons of particular towns in Ecuador. Pablo refers to the patron virgins of other towns, and Miguel says the Our Father and Hail Mary prayers during his ritual.

Another source of power comes from the oriente region. As I described in chapter 6, the oriente is perceived as a repository of ancient indigenous knowledge. For some healers the black shiny stones, which are also used by Canelos shamans (N. Whitten 1976, 1985), represent this power. Luis, a man who was an apprentice to a shaman who is now deceased, told me that his mentor would call on the Aushiris during his healing rituals. *Aushiris* is an old term, rarely used today, to refer to a distant Amazonian people, the Huaorani (also called Tahua or Ahua Schiri, see N. Whitten 1976). Miguel was also familiar with the name Aushiris; he said they were a people from deep in the forest, and "even the women carried spears." Another shaman, Byron, had several ancient objects (which he called *museoguna*, "museums" or "zoos") and artifacts from the Amazonian region, including monkey skulls and jaguar skins, as part of his mesa.

A Shaman's Prayer to the Mountain Mother

After cleansing their patients, shamans go to the sacred mountain shrines to leave offerings. For some illnesses, the shaman makes an offering to Quinchi Urcu or the contiguous mountain Palama (also referred to as Palama Cruz) after the ritual. Offerings include live guinea pigs, dolls made from a burro bone, oranges, and red chili peppers. The doll is used for sick children, and should be dressed in a tiny poncho for a sick boy or tiny *anaco* (skirt) for a sick girl, or swaddled (*maytu*) for a baby. The child should sleep with the doll, hugging it close to his or her chest, and the shaman should go, ideally in the middle of the night, to leave it at the shrines in Quinchi Urcu (also called Mama Quinchi) or Palama.

In 1992 I recorded an offering prayer that Manuel made to Quinchi Urcu. He had cleansed a sick little boy and made a doll from a burro bone. The child was to sleep hugging the doll close to his chest, and he and his mother were to come the next morning to go with Manuel to Quinchi Urcu to pray that the child recover. Although the mother failed to show up, Manuel went to leave an offering of a candle and coins and pray that the boy recover. I accompanied him to record the ritual, and another man went along because he was under pressure to finish an order of tapestries to deliver to a store in Quito. He brought some thread to leave as an offering to Mama Quinchi so that he would weave faster and complete the order on time.

Before heading up the hill to Quinchi Urcu, Manuel stopped at Cruz Pamba to "bathe" in the sacred dirt, which he said was *yaculaya*, like water. This was before the alcaldes had placed a cross there in 1994, so it was just a crossroads of sacred ground. Figure 7.2 shows Manuel "bathing" in the sacred dirt, and one can see the used medicinal plant bundles that others have left scattered around the sacred site. From Cruz Pamba one walks up the hill Catitagua to Quinchi Urcu. At the top of Quinchi Urcu, there is a patch of achupalla plants that forms a natural shelter over a hole in the mountain where offerings can be left. There, Manuel said the following prayer:

> Virgin of Quinchi, Mama Quinchi, Dear little Mama Quinchi, Virgin of Mama Quinchi, Tungurahua, Mama Ahuila, Chimba Urcu [Palama], Mama Quinchi [he then recited the Lord's Prayer], Father Sun, Father Moon, please watch over [him], please make him become healthy [*sanayachibangui*]. See now I'm paying, with coins, with a candle. [He buried the offerings in the hole.]

Manuel explained that we would leave only half the offering at this shrine, which was the "female." The other candle and coin would be left at another shrine on the mountain, the "male" shrine, yet this dual gender division was contained within the overall mountain mother, gendered feminine. Others classify the shrines as "old" versus "young." Manuel always takes one road to the mountain to leave the offering and a different

FIGURE 7.2. Manuel "bathes" in the sacred earth at Cruz Pamba in 1992, before the cross (shown in figure 1.2) was placed there.

road back, just as people do when they leave offerings at Cruz Pamba. The term "Mama Ahuila," meaning "grandmother," is a respectful term Salasacans use for the volcano Tungurahua.

Life Histories of Shamanic Calling

Most Salasacan shamans are men, but I did meet two female shamans. One was Manuel's daughter-in-law, who was just beginning her call to healing at the time of my research. The other was Teresa, who received the gift of healing after she had a near-death experience. She was very ill after giving birth, and God revealed himself to her. According to Teresa, God came down from Palama to Cruz Pamba, and there he showed her two roads. God said, "Look, there is the cauldron [*paila*] of hell. Think well. Do you want to go to the cauldron, or do you want to be saved? Those who believe in me will be saved." He then showed her all the medicinal plants in the world that were good for healing and told her to pray to him at 12:00 noon and 12:00 midnight. After four years she would be called upon to heal. But God warned her not to charge a lot of money to her clients.

Now when she heals she uses medicinal plants from Teligote, and boils rocks from twelve different springs in water, giving that water to patients. She said that a sick child should sleep with a bone doll for five days, wearing the same clothes. The doll is swaddled like a baby and is "named" (*shutichi*, the same word that means "baptized"). Then at 12:00 midnight she must go with the child to Palama Cruz. At Palama Cruz they leave a guinea pig dressed in twelve colored ribbons, "so that the rainbow takes" the sickness. She leaves the bone doll and twelve kinds of food, including hominy, pork, and oranges. She brings water and maize beer in traditional clay vessels to leave at the mountain. She also leaves twelve types of herbs. I asked why she had to pray at 12:00 midnight and 12:00 noon, and she said, "Those are God's times." I asked why she had to leave twelve "classes" of every offering, and she replied, "Because that works." "God takes away the sickness when you go with twelve." Then she added, "But only with faith, only believing in God."

All the shamans I interviewed depend on the powers of the sacred landscape. Teresa's ability to cure people depends on her having faith in God, using the right herbal remedies, using stones to represent sacred springs, and leaving the right number of offerings at Palama Cruz. Manuel's healing rituals depend on geography in two ways. First, he calls on the shadows of powerful mountains throughout Ecuador to aid him in the healing ritual, and on the yumbos from lowland regions to the east and west of the Andes. Second, he bathes in the sacred dirt above Cruz Pamba and leaves offerings to Quinchi Urcu in order to appropriate the power of local places to heal his patients. Pablo also leaves offerings on Quinchi Urcu after a healing ritual.

Traditionally, novices would sleep in local sacred places in order to gain shamanic powers. The sleep state, a liminal period in which people are vulnerable to soul-stealing mountains, is also the state in which people can gain powers from mountains. Places where men have slept to become shamans include the mountains Quinchi Urcu and Teligote. Others report that shamans bathe in local sacred springs. For example, when Luis was training as an apprentice to a shaman his mentor told him to sleep by the enchanted lake on the mountain Teligote: "He told me that to become a jambij [shaman] I had to spend the night on Teligote, in the middle of the forest, at the lake. He said that he spent the night there, and a shadow gave him a red palm wood stick. From spending the night there he said he became a jambij." But Luis never completed his training.

Byron, a healer who was in his sixties when I interviewed him in 1997, reported that his father used to beat his mother when she was pregnant with him. When he was in his mother's womb, she fell asleep in Yuruq Allpa (a sector close to Salasaca). There, he cried three times (in the womb). He was born with some powers to divine but, because his father fed pig fat to his mother while she was pregnant, his powers were not very strong. If she hadn't eaten pig fat, which is believed to neutralize shamanic powers, he would have been born with very strong powers to divine.

Jaime, a man in his sixties, told me that he and his brother decided to sleep on Quinchi Urcu in order to become shamans. There, he had a dream that someone gave him two red shawls and two white shawls. After the dreams his body was aching. He began to dream again, and the dream told him, "Get a live guinea pig and cure yourself." Everything appeared in the guinea pig (after it had been killed, skinned, and disemboweled): the fever, the pain, and the sickness. There he learned how to heal. In the same dreams medicines were revealed to him. He still receives knowledge in dreams that tell him how to heal through medicinal plants and massage. But the dreams also tell him, "Don't charge people a lot of money for your services."

Another man explained to me that when a person sleeps on a mountain a being appears, called Tayta (father) Quinchi Urcu. This happens "in a dream," or some say that the being "causes a dream" or "leaves a dream" (sueño shitan). For women, he said, a female being appears, but I do not know of any women who have slept on the mountain.

Janet, a woman who was in her late teens when I interviewed her in 1998, said her (deceased) father was a healer. Her father reportedly received powers from the Patate River. He threw two oranges and two pieces of bread into the river. Instead of carrying them away, the river sent them back to him. He took them home, and from then on he felt that he had the power to heal and began gathering stones. He found one particular stone when he went to cure someone in the town of Quero. He was throwing away the used medicinal plants in the gorge, and there he found a large stone that was good for healing.

Juan Luis, whose late uncle Juan Chango had been a great shaman in the 1950s, told me:

> Juan Chango was able to divine since he was a child. When his mother used to go to the market in Pelileo, he would read in his palm and say, "Now my mother is coming down the road, she's coming down this road with the food." His mother, fearing that the army would draft him for his divinatory powers, gave him pig fat and pig meat to make him lose powers. But when he got older, a woman made him dream [soñachiga]. She appeared from Cruz Pamba and said, "Come bringing fruit [oranges and plantains], you will become a healer again, it is time for you to begin your work, the patrones [mountains] are calling you." The woman was a servant of the mountains. He went to sleep at Cruz Pamba with the woman, but in his visions there was a house there that only he could see. The power was from the mountain Catitagua. He became one of the most powerful shamans in Salasaca.
>
> The army drafted him. First they put him through a test. They buried weapons, rifles, and blindfolded him to see if he could guess where they were. He did, and as it was the time of the Ecuadorian-Peruvian war, they kept him there to divine where the enemy's arms were hidden. But he escaped and came home. He was killed due to sorcery (other healers were envious).

Shamanic traditions from various cultures involve marriage to spirit husbands or wives (Lewis 1971). The nature of the spiritual marriage varies according to local cultural traditions. For example, among the Chilean Mapuche both male and female shamans become spiritual brides who "seduce and call their *filew*—at once husband and master—to possess their heads and grant them knowledge" (Bacigalupo 2007:87). They do this by donning the feminine attire that represents "wifeliness" to the spirit. Bacigalupo shows that Mapuche shamans take on gendered ritual relationships independent of their anatomical sex. Among the Ecuadorian Amazonian Napo Runa, men depend on female spirit owners to release game and fish so that they can provide for their families, and some engage in sexual relations with female spirits in dreams. According to Michael Uzendoski (2005:128) "hunters occupy a subordinate position in this relation, and they are in no position to demand things of the spirit women."

The story of Juan Chango's spirit-wife, with whom he would sleep at Cruz Pamba, attests to his special connection with the spirit world through an affinal relationship, although this was the only Salasacan case of spirit-marriage that I heard of. The story provides another example of the way places communicate to people through dreams, since the spirit woman "made him dream" and called him to come sleep with her at their spirit-house in Cruz Pamba.

In 1959 the anthropologists Piedad Peñaherrera de Costales and Alfredo Costales Samaniego described their interview with Juan Chango. They reported that he had a glass "magic bottle" which contained a replica of Christ's crown. He claimed that the bottle was "born" in a mountain. Chango told the Ecuadorian anthropologists that he did not gain his powers from mountains but had power because he cried in his mother's womb (Peñaherrera de Costales and Costales Samaniego 1959). Still, his nephew's description of him sleeping in Cruz Pamba indicates the role of sacred places in the manifestation of his congenital power. Juan Chango also possessed ancient stones and hatchet-shaped stones, and he had stones representing "mountain mothers" (1959:52).

The Costales reported the practice of shamans going to Quinchi Urcu to leave guinea pigs and cups of water representing twelve clay vessels of maize beer on the mountain, asking the mountain to "give back the soul" of the patient. Their informants told them that Quinchi Urcu is the dwelling place of the rainbow. During my fieldwork in the 1990s, I did not hear of such an association, but some people believe that the rainbow is a sign of an impending death in the community.

The preceding cases show that shamans have special knowledge of geographic locations with powers and serve as mediators between the body of the sick person and the powers of the landscape to restore health. Shamans nurture a relationship with the landscape, the source of their healing powers. They also serve to interpret illness for the patients in terms of the landscape and thereby influence the way others think about the landscape. Shamans serve as practitioners of some of the most widespread aspects of native South American religious practice. Their beliefs and rites are rooted in an ancient understanding of a relationship between humans and sacred places, and they engage in reciprocal exchanges with the mountain mothers in order to heal their clients.

Shamanism and Religion

As ritual specialists, shamans must be knowledgeable of the workings of the spiritual world. Since I am analyzing shamanism as an enduring aspect of native religious practices, it is important to present both the ritual specialists' understanding of cosmology as well as the understandings of those who have had experiences with shamans. I spoke with many people about their experiences with shamans and about their understanding of the cosmological basis of shamanic ritual efficacy. I will present here only a sample of some of those interviews.

Manuel gave this account of his patient who had suffered from dizzy spells:

> MANUEL: When he was a child his parents went somewhere and he fell asleep in the road. At that time the mountain got him. He went crazy. He has the falling sickness, a falling attack. It had his soul; it caught his soul, took it.
> RC: Who?
> MANUEL: The mountain. The mountain from that side. That's where he was sleeping. At that time they didn't cure him right away. He was now beginning to go crazy. It was making his head hurt; he was with an aching heart. The devils had kicked him in the heart. The impurities, the sicknesses. It was a long time that he had been falling down, more than seven years. It was persecuting him [catin], consuming his body. Right now he had headaches and heartaches, and he had only passed out. But if he hadn't been cured he would have started saying crazy things.

In this case Manuel explains the ataque as the result of the mountain taking the patient's soul and persecuting the patient. Although he uses the term "devils" to describe the bad spirits "kicking" the patient's heart, the mountains are not associated with devils in the Christian sense of evil beings from hell. The principal cause of the illness was the mountain from that particular hamlet. Sara, the patient's sister-in-law, was present during the healing ritual, and I asked how the ritual worked according to her understanding:

> He had an ataque. With the stones, the candle, the trago, and all the plants, he is becoming better. The stones are powerful-like [poderoso

laya]. Calling, the shaman moves a person's illness away. Naming the stones, the stones indicate where it [the soul] was taken. The shaman has the mind [Sp. *mente*], he concentrates, and the stones indicate to him where it [the soul] is. The stones are powerful, like God [*Dios-malaya*]. The stones indicated that the ataque happened up there, up from the house, and it's true. When he was a baby he fainted. The shaman told us that if the healing ritual didn't work, we would have to go back to that place and get his spirit [*espíritu*], his soul [*alma*], from the place. But the ritual worked.

Sara understood the cause of the cure as a combination of the power of the stones and the mind-power of the shaman. For all these powers she used the Spanish words for "powerful," "mind," and "concentration." The closest Quichua words would be *yuyana*, meaning "thought," or *alli yuyana*, "to think well," and some have used these terms to describe how shamans cure. But many, like Sara, use Spanish words for power [*poder*], God [*Dios*], and mental concentration [*concentración*] to describe religious phenomena.

Juan Luis reported:

My son was sick when he was little. Manuel went with me at 4:00 a.m. to Achupalla [Quinchi Urcu]. After we cleansed my son with eggs and candles, and after he slept with a burro bone doll, we went. First we went to the cemetery, and in the corner where the first person was buried in the cemetery after they built it, we buried two eggs. The first person buried there has power [*fuerza*], he was a centenarian and the *huañusha causaric* people [those who have had near-death experiences] say that they saw the cemetery as a town and he was governing the cemetery.

Then we took dirt from the middle of the cemetery. Then we went to Cruz Pamba. We left a candle and eggs in the hole, where there used to be a lot of century plants, and we took dirt from there. Then we went to where there is another hole on the road to Pelileo [the hole called] Imbabura, and we took dirt from there. Then we went to Quinchi Urcu. It was dark and rainy, and there was a rainbow. Manuel said it was the jealousy of the mountain; the mountain didn't want us to get any closer. So he blew trago and cinnamon in the direction of

Quinchi Urcu, and the rainbow disappeared within about ten minutes. We went to Quinchi, and there he named my son and said [to the mountain], "Victor . . . is your son, make this son grow well, like a century plant make him grow well." Then Manuel whistled and sang to the mountains from the four sides. We left the burro bone and we also took dirt from Quinchi Urcu. When we got home, he told me to boil the dirt from the four places [the cemetery, Cruz Pamba, Imbabura hole, and Quinchi Urcu] together. I had to wait until the water cleared, and then my son had to drink it. By drinking this water little by little every day, my son got better. There is some power [poder], a force [fuerza] like sami.

In this case, Juan Luis's own understanding of cosmology comes from the teachings of the shaman Manuel. Based on his experience of his son being healed, Juan Luis can testify to the power of sacred places, contained in the dirt from those places. He compares the power to the life essence called sami, which is also mentioned in the Quichua ceremonial blessings (chap. 4). The dirt was taken from the cemetery, where people are buried underground, and from holes in the ground at sacred places. The cemetery and the holes represent access to underworld and chthonic powers. Throughout the pre-Columbian Americas, elites used symbols of conduits to the underworld to represent access to chthonic power (Gillespie 1993; Lathrap 1985). Stories of the appearance of saints from within the earth or the trunks of plants and trees (described in chaps. 2 and 4) further reinforce the concept of power emanating from within the earth. Both Shamanic practices and individual offerings (described in chap. 8) depend on crossroads, holes, and crevices to tap into chthonic powers.

Another source for Juan Luis's understanding of cosmology is the group of people who have had near-death experiences, called *huañusha causariccuna* in Salasaca. According to Juan Luis, in near-death experiences people have seen that the first Salasacan to be buried in the cemetery (built in the late 1960s) is powerful, both politically and spiritually. People say he was a centenarian, which places him at the top of Andean age hierarchies.

Another woman, Gladys, explained that after the shaman makes the initial diagnosis by cleansing with a guinea pig and examining its organs, he arranges for the healing session. Gladys said that during the session the shaman uses healing stones and calls on the powers of the mountain fathers, mountain mothers, and lightning. The mountains and the lightning, she said, carry the sickness away. A young man named Esteban explained that people leave guinea pigs on the mountain as offerings, so that the mountain will restore the soul of a sick child. Sometimes it works, but sometimes it doesn't. He knew a couple that did this after medical doctors failed to heal their child, but neither scientific medicine nor shamanism worked, and the child died. The explanations of these nonspecialists show that shamanic practice is based on a shared cosmology of the powers of sacred places, especially mountains.

Cultural models of illness and medicine in Ecuador incorporate both scientific medicine and traditional healing of both Iberian and native Andean origin. Among the recent political declarations of the indigenous political organization CONAIE is a demand for fair, humanitarian treatment of all peoples (indigenous and nonindigenous) in hospitals and clinics, as well as respect for indigenous shamans and traditional medicine (CONAIE 1997: 44–45). There are indigenous people with medical degrees (two in Salasaca), and there are blanco-mestizos who go to indigenous shamans. People use both models of illness with no conflict. Dorothea S. Whitten (2003) shows that the health network in Ecuador is based on a "multinational paradigm." In her analysis of paintings of shamanic rituals by indigenous artists from Tigua, she describes a painting that depicts a patient in a Red Cross clinic being treated by a nurse. Many indigenous people have used such clinics, and many others would like to have medical clinics in their communities. This does not conflict with indigenous beliefs in shamanism: to the contrary, it represents the intercultural nature of Andean indigenous societies and the value of foreign knowledge.

The symbolic value of foreign knowledge relates to perceptions of Amazonia. By naming different regions of Ecuador and calling on other indigenous peoples from lowland provinces beyond the Andes, the Salasacan shamans show some control of distant knowledge and power (Helms 1988). One young shaman has both a nursing degree and first aid certificate from a city school as well as a degree in shamanism from the Association of Indigenous Shamans of Napo (Amazonian Ecuador). This course included instruction in taking ayahuasca, the hallucinogenic drink of lowland shamans.

In addition to the multimodal nature of Ecuadorian health paradigms, people use metaphors drawn from hospitals to explain indigenous medicine. Luis said that cleansing with a guinea pig is like taking an x-ray, but better, because everything appears in the internal organs of the guinea pig. He also said that after the body is cleansed and the plant bundles thrown in the crossroads, the patient becomes stronger, "as if an injection had been given, as if medicine had been taken" (*shug inyección churashcalaya, jarabe ubishcalaya*).

Conclusion

Modern shamanic practices reflect religious transculturation based on veneration of sacred places, historical contact between people of different regions, exchange of ritual knowledge, and incorporation of Catholic prayers with supplications to the mountain mother. Shamans act as mediators between cultural knowledge and individual experience as well as between the body and the landscape. The healing ritual involves the shaman communicating and working with the mountains in order to cure the patient. The shaman also leaves offerings as payment to the sacred mountain known as Mama Quinchi and says special prayers to the mountain mother on behalf of the clients. Salasacan shamans draw on the local and distant geography of Ecuador to manipulate the powers of Amazonia and the Andes Mountains in order to heal the bodies of individual clients.

The practice of shamanism in Salasaca reflects the persistence of native Andean religion through historical transformations, including the archbishop's call in 1885 to purge the parish of "sorcerers." Despite church efforts to eradicate shamanism, a continuing shamanic network, probably dating to pre-Columbian times, thrives throughout Ecuador. Salasacan shamans are knowledgeable ritual specialists who deal with mountain spirits and the spirits of powerful yumbos from the lowland forest regions. Salasacan individuals also leave offerings to sacred places. Up to this point I have focused on religion as the result of historical processes and religious specialists, but religion cannot be separated from the individual experiences of those who practice it. In the next chapter I present the narratives of individual Salasacans as they tell of their religious experiences.

CHAPTER 8

Narrating the Sacred Landscape

Religious Ethnographies of the Particular

Atuntaqui, 1792
Having gone [to the mountain Imbabura] to gather firewood, because
she was curious she arrived where there were voices, and Christian
prayers and songs, to a spot where more than a hundred souls were
gathered, to complain about the drought they were experiencing, my
wife got mixed up in it, which was the cause of this rigorous punishment [one hundred public lashings].

Salasaca, 1998
I remember it like this. There in Quinchi Urcu, when it hadn't rained
for a while, they held a fiesta. The people went carrying water in puños
and in pondos [types of ceramic vessels] to pour it there, so that it
would rain. We poured it in the achupalla plants on Quinchi Urcu.
There had just been sun, day after day. The old ones said, "Let's go! It
hasn't rained. Let's all go to pour water in the achupalla. It's just been
sunny every day." Everyone went, saying "Let's go" and carried water.
[They went] to pour the water. . . . They poured the water there, and
one or two days later it just rained. Upon putting the water there it
rained. . . . God made it rain. Upon seeing the water placed in the
mountain he made it rain. The people placed the water there saying,
"Please make it rain, it hasn't rained at all. We can't sow any crops.
There is nothing." In this way, asking God, we put the water and it just
rained. Since long ago the old ones would have fiestas there so that it
would rain, and it would just rain. Putting water there it rains, that's
what the old ones would say. Having heard that, we also said "Let's go
put water there" when it didn't rain, we went too.

IN 1792 A NATIVE OF ATUNTAQUI, in northern Ecuador, filed a formal complaint against his parish priest. The priest had publicly punished the man's wife for practicing "idolatry" on the mountain Imbabura. According to the petitioner, Juan Paulino Carlosama, his wife got mixed up with a large group of people who had gathered on the mountain to pray because of a drought, and the parish priest punished his wife unjustly (cited in Moreno Yánez 1991:535–36).

In contemporary Salasaca, older people recall experiencing a severe drought, which ended after they gathered to pray on Quinchi Urcu. Although Marta indicated that people no longer pray collectively on the mountain, many people continue to go on an individual basis to petition Mama Quinchi for favors. Furthermore, narratives of the collective rain-making ritual serve as a basis for individual decisions to leave a mountain offering. Such individual religious practices are the subject of this chapter, and the actions of modern Salasacans show the form that Andean mountain worship takes today.

Narrative Ethnographies of the Particular

In her essay "Writing against Culture," Lila Abu-Lughod advocates writing "ethnographies of the particular" in the form of narrative life histories as a way to overcome generalization and "Othering." Ethnographies of the particular also have the benefit of showing how larger national and transnational processes and cultural institutions are lived out by real individuals: "the effects of extralocal and long-term processes are only manifested locally and specifically, produced in the actions of individuals living their particular lives, inscribed in their bodies and in their words" (Abu-Lughod 1991:150). In order to understand what "Andean religion" means, it is necessary to understand how this religion is lived and experienced by real individuals. Although I do not present complete biographies, I do present the narratives of men and women, young and old, literate and nonliterate people. An analysis of the narrative expressions of such experiences allows us to move beyond an essentialized paradigm of Andean symbol systems to understand the meanings of such symbols at the level of individual belief and experience. The anecdotes I present here show that sacred geography, as an important aspect of Andean cosmology, is not just a pre-Columbian survival but a part of lived experience that is continuously re-created by human agents. I especially focus on the role of individual experience in maintaining, re-creating, and questioning beliefs about the efficacy of sacred places. Salasacans recognize and accept a multiplicity of personal experiences with the landscape.

By stressing the multivocality of Salasacans one can avoid what Orin Starn (1991) has termed "Andeanism." According to Starn, the logic of Andeanism "dichotomizes between the Occidental, coastal, urban, and mestizo and the non-Western, highland, rural, and indigenous; it then essentializes the highland side of the equation to talk about 'lo andino,' 'the Andean worldview,' 'indigenous highland culture,' or, in more old-fashioned formulations, 'the Andean mind' or 'the Andean Indians'" (Starn 1991:66). According to Starn, part of the problem with earlier ethnographic representations of Andean peasants was the "limited focus" of research dominated by theories of ecological symbolism and ritual. A focus on individual experience allows us to overcome a static view of Andean cosmology and show instead that Salasacan cosmology accommodates doubt and skepticism but also validates individual beliefs and experiences.

Near-Death Experiences

Narratives of near-death experiences are one of the most compelling examples of how the historical experience of colonial evangelization projects impinged on individual consciousness. People who have had near-death experiences tell of their souls traveling the landscape, from Cruz Pamba to the "grandmother" volcano Tungurahua, and they tell how these geographic features appear in the other life. Modern near-death experiences in Salasaca may have roots in an older Andean conception of life-passage and ancestorhood: "Many Andean elders, as they approach the passage to ancestor status, undergo episodes of unconsciousness considered temporary deaths (Zuidema and Quispe 1973). Stereotyped narratives about these experiences are common. They generally include a stagewise journey at whose end the elder is bidden to stay a while longer among the living" (Salomon 1995:328). Peter Wogan (2004) recorded a story of a near-death experience in Salasaca that is a clear example of this pattern: a man underwent all the stages of the journey to the afterlife until God checked a book of names and told him his time had not yet come, and that he should stay in this life longer. Here, I analyze near-death experience narratives as a reflection of the transculturation of religious imagery. Such narratives have created an association between Cruz Pamba and purgatory, a Catholic concept of being in an in-between state that is neither heaven nor hell.

Near-death experiences occur under varying circumstances, including accidents, illness, and fainting spells. People who have had such experiences are referred to collectively as huañusha causariccuna or *huañusha vueltaccuna*, both terms referring to a person who temporarily died and came back to life. Although individual reports vary, people often refer to stories told by the huañusha causariccuna when describing the sacred landscape and the afterlife. The most common image described in such narratives is that of a giant, four-handled cauldron, such as the one depicted in Eurocentric colonial paintings of hell. Those who say they have seen the landscape in the afterlife locate the boiling cauldron, or a lake of fire, at Cruz Pamba. According to one man, the old people used to refer to Cruz Pamba as *chaupimundo*, "the middle world," because it was "like purgatory." Narratives of near-death experiences illustrate indigenous interpretations of Roman Catholic imagery.

Purgatory, as a "third place" between heaven and hell, became part of official church teaching in the twelfth century (Le Goff 1984:3). Purgatory was a place where souls underwent a trial, a place where they were purged of their sins before they entered heaven. Given that purgatory was a place of transition, it makes sense that in the Andes it would be located geographically at the crossroads, on a part of the landscape that symbolizes a threshold. Gary Urton (1980) provides linguistic evidence for the relationship between crossroads and thresholds. In the southern Andes, the union or bifurcation of roads is called *chaca*. In various dialects of Quechua, the words *chaca* and *chacana* refer to crosses, the Christian crucifix, crossroads, thresholds, bridges, lintels, and ladders. The ladder and the bridge, which are symbols of a trial in the afterlife in medieval European cosmology, are linguistically linked to crossroads in southern Quechua dialects in the Andes, further corroborating the association of crossroads with a threshold. I will present here one narrative of a woman who had a near-death experience. Since the modern Salasacan cemetery is near Cruz Pamba, the narrator uses the word *cemetery* when referring to the area around the crossroads:

A worm crawled into my ear. *I died.* I didn't feel anything. I saw those witches carrying *sucus* [tall bamboo plants] behind them. They appeared "in" my eyes clearly. [Her son adds "in her thoughts."] Then from that Cruz Pamba cemetery, you know, around back where the festival dancers enter, there is a *big* cauldron, a four-handled cauldron, where the witches are. There is a witch stirring with a big spoon. In the back/east crossroads, in the place where the festival dancers enter, that's where the witch appeared cooking those that practiced witchcraft. Then, at the ground down from the cemetery, just down from the cemetery, there is a plain with a lake. There is a lot of water on the ground, a lake ground, *water*, an *ocean*. But it doesn't appear now, it appeared when I died. My soul saw it. Dying, I really saw everything. Just like a lake, a lot of water, like the sea. It was too big to fit within the scope of one's vision [*pambundig*]. I died and I saw on the ground down from that cross, in that *cross* where the dancers enter, down from there is a *big* cauldron, with an indigenous woman, but a witch, stirring the people, Salasacans, that practiced witchcraft, with a big spoon. Then for some reason I came back to life.

When the narrator says "it doesn't appear now" she uses the word *cunun*, "for now." This word choice indicates that in the here and now, this world, the lake does not appear, but that the landscapes exists in an alternate form in the other time-space. This alternative reality figured in the shamanic experience of Juan Chango (chap. 7), in which he had a house and spirit-wife located at Cruz Pamba. Another man told me the details of his grandmother's near-death experience, and he painted a picture of what his grandmother described as the Salasacan landscape in the afterlife (fig. 8.1). The painting shows the convergence of roads at Cruz Pamba, where there is a lake of fire and the cauldron. The volcano Tungurahua appears in the distance, where the souls travel. The artist noted that before the Salasacan cemetery was built in the 1960s, pallbearers would have to carry coffins all the way to Pelileo. They would avoid walking directly over the "fire lake" at Cruz Pamba, and would instead walk on the slope of Catitagua to avoid this spot. His painting shows this alternative path.

The spatialization of purgatory in Andean Ecuador occurred through historical ideological processes in which popular folk beliefs, sacred

FIGURE 8.1. A Salasacan artist's depiction of the landscape in the afterlife, based on his grandmother's narrative of her near-death experience. Note the lake of fire where the roads meet at Cruz Pamba and the volcano Tungurahua, where souls travel.

geography, and symbols from various Old World traditions were appropriated by the Catholic Church, became official church teaching, and were then incorporated into the symbol system, sacred geography, and folklore of Andean indigenous peoples. Although the church today maintains that purgatory is a state of being rather than a place (Le Goff 1984:13), older discourses located the entrances to hell and purgatory geographically.

In Salasaca, part of the colonial imagery of hell was grafted onto an indigenous sacred landscape and incorporated into representations of the afterlife. The punishments at the cauldron of the sacred crossroads are for sins against Salasacan moral teachings. Narratives of near-death experiences not only provide information about the sacred landscape but may also enforce moral values. The cauldron, witchcraft, devils, and sacred geography are part of the indigenous world, shaped by powerful images and historical experience. The narratives of near-death experiences show how Catholic indoctrination shaped individual experiences with death. Narrative is the vehicle through which the imagery and symbolism of personal experiences become part of the collective body of discourse that reproduces this imagery and symbolism.

Near-death experiences, soul loss, and illness are things that happen to the body against one's will. But Salasacans also exercise agency in their relationship with the local landscape. They leave offerings at sacred places to petition God or the mountain mother for certain favors. Their decision to do so is based on knowledge passed on in the form of narratives. These narratives tell of the powers of particular places, and individuals draw on this knowledge in their own experiences with the sacred places. The continued practice of leaving offerings and uttering supplications to sacred places maintains subjective, sacred places, as opposed to objective, neutral spaces, a distinction made by several theorists (Casey 1996; Hirsch 1995; Relph 1976; Tuan 1977). People who have personal, embodied religious experiences with places tell their stories, and those stories become part of the collective body of knowledge that shapes perceptions of the landscape. People who share these stories constitute what Lawrence Taylor calls an interpretive community. They contribute to the discourse of sacred places and create a "field of religious experience" (Taylor 1995:243). In the next section I present narratives of individual experiences with the landscape. These individual stories shed light on the meaning of "sacred places" at the level of individual belief and consciousness.

Lived Religion

Robert Anthony Orsi (2002) uses the term "lived religion" to promote an approach to studying religion as people experience it in particular situations. A visit to local place shrines reveals what a general term such as *sacred geography* means in practice (fig. 8.2). I undertook many trips to Salasaca during intermittent fieldwork between 1991 and 2008, and whenever I visited Quinchi Urcu, Palama, or Cruz Pamba, I always found fresh offerings left there by recent, anonymous petitioners. In chapter 7 I mentioned that a weaver accompanied the shaman (in 1991) to leave bundles of wool yarn at a shrine on Quinchi Urcu in order to weave tapestries quickly. This is an offering I have seen commonly over the years. Peter Wogan (2004) analyzes the connection between weaving and writing in mountain offerings. People leave notebooks and pens, as well as little spindle whorls and wool, at mountain shrines in order to master difficult skills. I have also seen occasional letters or pictorial representations left at the same shrines as petitions to the mountain mother. One of these said, "Mama Quinchi, I deliver to you my heart and soul." This note was most likely used for love magic, since the letter had a man's name written on it. Another time I saw a piece of paper requesting a happy marriage, a house, and money, with a picture (drawn with colored pens) of a happy Salasacan man and woman inside a home. The mountain not only gives talent and "guides" weavers and musicians, but it can work on people's emotional states, causing desire for another person or the motivation to work.

There are other sacred places in Salasaca. For example, a hidden lake in the forest at the top of the mountain Teligote is rumored to contain treasures. A statue of San Antonio is housed in a small chapel on the mountain, and it is said the couple who sponsors a fiesta in his honor will have abundant crops and livestock. Punta Rumi is a large, "ugly," dangerous rock located in the gorge. This is the only sacred place that is associated mainly with negative powers. Rumor has it that a shaman slept there to gain powers, but he went mad. Others claim that they went mad after resting near the rock and had their senses restored only after leaving offerings to the rock and drinking an infusion of dirt and scrapings from the rock. These powerful places are part of the lived experience of Salasacan religiosity, but here I will focus on the complex of sacred places near the border of Salasaca and the town of Pelileo: Quinchi Urcu, the

FIGURE 8.2. Offerings left at the shrine of achupalla plants on Quinchi Urcu. Manuel left the candles after praying to the mountain mother. Scattered clothing, spindle whorls, and other offerings remain from previous, anonymous petitioners.

mountain that is part of a series of connected, sacred hills; and Cruz Pamba, the hole that runs underground at the crossroads at the foot of those sacred hills.

I will provide brief biographical sketches of the people I interviewed. Sara is a young woman who as of 2008 is married and has a child. She sells crafts at the small market in Salasaca and she worked briefly as a housekeeper in the city. Her brother, Julio, worked in Otavalo for some time when he was a teenager. He is an excellent weaver and made many of the tapestries that the Otavalans sold to tourists. Indeed, many of the tapestries sold by Otavalans were produced by Salasacan weavers. Julio is also a talented musician, and he traveled to the United States with his Andean folkloric musical group.

Sara, who was in her early twenties at the time I interviewed her in 1998, told me about a time when she used the mountain: "I went about five years ago with my mother. We pulled out some hair from the cow and wool from the sheep and wrapped it around a candle. We left it there, you know, up in Quinchi Urcu, in the crevice. It worked! Both the cow and the sheep gave birth."

I asked her how it worked. She replied, "I don't know how it works. Seeing that in the past they did it like this, we did it. But it really did work, doing that, the animals gave birth. The candle burns there. . . . From the mountain it works. There must be something almost like God there." Sara and her mother went to Quinchi Urcu because they knew that the older generations had used it before them. Their own experience with their animals giving birth after the offering confirms for them the power of the mountain to help the animals breed.

Sara's brother, Julio, also used the mountain. When he was a teenager, he wanted to let his hair grow long the way other successful Ecuadorian folk musicians did. He decided to cut his hair and leave it in the crevice on Quinchi Urcu so that it would grow. He explained his reason for doing so:

> My grandfather [mother's father] told me about how they went to Quinchi Urcu, long ago, during the drought. They went with drums and flutes to make rain, and sure enough it rained shortly after, like the next day or something. They took hominy and maize beer to cry out, like a rite, but they made a little fiesta. It was like a minga; they called all the people to come bringing food. So I got the idea to leave my hair, in the hole there. My grandfather told me that people go there for anything: in order to work well, women go so that their husbands won't have affairs, they cleanse animals with a candle so that they don't get sick and so that they grow fast and get big. My grandfather said that anything one wants one has to pray there and it will be accomplished. I also went with my band and we prayed and played music there [in order to become successful musicians]. . . . My grandfather says that if you believe, your faith, your thoughts, will carry you and you can achieve your desire by going to Quinchi Urcu.

When I asked him if the offering worked for growing his hair, he said "of course," so I asked what explanation people give for how it works. Julio replied, "From experience they know it works. People always say that Quinchi Urcu is a sacred place." Julio, like his sister, drew on the knowledge of an older generation in deciding to use the mountain. This is an example of how people re-create religion through individual acts:

although he had not heard of other people leaving hair on Quinchi Urcu, he was innovative in his attempt to grow his hair. He referred specifically to the collective rain-making ritual that older generations talk about. This event is a salient reference for people when I ask them about Quinchi Urcu: their parents and grandparents told them about how they left water on the mountain, and soon thereafter it rained. Young and old people use the experience as evidence of the potential power of the mountain, so Julio got the idea to leave his hair there. Julio also emphasized the role that mental processes—faith, belief, and thoughts—play in the efficacy of the prayers and offerings made on the mountain. For Julio, as for his sister, their experience serves as further evidence that the mountain offering has accomplished their desires.

Another young man, Esteban, exemplifies the relationship between the public symbolism of discourse about a powerful mountain and the private symbolism of dreams (Firth 1973). Esteban married his girlfriend when he was quite young (late teens). Their son was a year old at the time (1992), and Esteban migrated to the United States shortly after the wedding. He worked in a pizzeria for a year and sent money home to his wife to pay for construction of a cement-block house on his parents' land. Like Julio, he belonged to a band of folkloric musicians. Esteban also wanted to be a good musician, and he also drew on the experience of older generations in using the mountain to meet his individual goals. He prayed at both of the crevices on Quinchi Urcu. In a 1998 interview he told me:

> There was a man, he is deceased now, but he was a really good flute player. He told me that he slept on Quinchi Urcu and someone appeared to him, dressed in red with black capes. That person [devil] played, and the man said, "I'll play until I win [play better]. He won, and that's how he became a really good flute player. . . . Having listened to the elders my brother and I went to Quinchi Urcu to sleep on the night of the full moon. They say that in that place . . . that a musician appears there, a devil who teaches musicians. The place with the little hole is called the "Grandfather" Quinchi. We left a stone in the hole there, at midnight, but nobody appeared to us! So we went to the part called "Baby" Quinchi and spent the night there. The next night it made me dream. I dreamed of a musician dressed in a white shirt and

black sweater with a black tie. He was there playing music in Baby Quinchi, the place where we had slept. He was a good panpipe player. When I told an elder about this dream, he said I should have gone to the place at that moment, to play better than him [the devil]. When you play better than the devil, he delivers the talent to you.

Again, I would emphasize here that *devil* (Sp. *diablo*) does not necessarily refer to an evil being in the European Christian tradition, but rather to a spirit. Esteban drew on information from elders both to get the idea to go to the mountain and to interpret his dream. The dream was the direct result of having slept on Quinchi Urcu, as reflected in the word *soñachiga*, "(he/she/it) made me dream." When I asked what or who made him dream, he said, "the musician in the dream." The association of musical talent with the spirit-owners of sacred places has been described for parts of Andean Peru, where musicians leave stringed instruments to be tuned by a mermaid—the female spirit-beings associated with a sacred water source (Turino 1983).

Not only do Salasacans have individual, subjective experiences with the collective symbolism of sacred places, but they also recognize the role of personal belief, the power of the mind, in producing such experiences. Salasacans acknowledge the role of faith in the efficacy of their rites, and they leave room for doubt and skepticism. Salasacans who have doubts about their own beliefs in the efficacy of mountain spirits still respect the experiences of others who strongly believe in the power of the mountain. For example, Raúl told me about the powers of the mountain, saying, "It's something powerful, that Quinchi. People who can't spin or weave . . . have you seen the hole?"

I answered "Yes, but how does it work?" He explained:

Faith. Faith and contact with the mountain. Nobody can beat it. They unite with the mountain, making a pact [Sp. *compacto*]. The musicians leave panpipes. People don't just leave distaffs there, but after cleansing sick people they leave well-dressed guinea pigs. The mountain, they say, works to make them better. If one believes in this mountain, it cleanses and makes one healthy again. [They leave] musical instruments, but small, just made [for this purpose], such as a little duct flute. The mountain has to become the guide, then . . .

Even the flute is guided. *Chilin*, it makes a finer sound and everything. If one really believes, they leave things there.

When I asked Raúl if he had ever left anything there, he first said no, but then he remembered:

Oh yeah! When my deceased mother was going to die we went with a jambij [shaman] after having cleansed her with a guinea pig. We went in the middle of the night to leave the guinea pig, but well dressed [wrapped in colored ribbons]. How scary! If one is too scared one could stay there, traumatized. The mountain takes. One has to go with courage. The shaman told us not to turn around and look back, the sickness would follow us. People still leave things there.

I persisted: "But do you believe in it?" Raúl's response to this question was interesting.

Well, you can see we haven't ever used it. And as my mother died anyway . . . I don't believe in it. But some, for some people, they really believe, and it must work. They also leave guinea pig droppings in order to have many guinea pigs. There must be something to it. There must be some reason that they leave it there. I have gone there in the day and seen many things. I think even to make people die they leave things. I see dolls; the shamans must leave them there, I think, it must be for sorcery. I wonder what they are for.

At this point, Raúl's wife recalled that people leave the dolls to heal sick children. Raúl's statement clearly shows skepticism, but by focusing on the power of individual belief, he does so in a way that does not undermine the overall system that attributes power to the mountain. In her study of Beng Earth worship Alma Gottlieb received a similar statement about the power of belief from a Beng priest, who told her that the Earth could bestow a special gift on her if she believed. As Gottlieb states, "we have an exceptionally sophisticated understanding of the role of individual mind in giving force to cultural symbols, and conversely an acknowledgment of the existence of doubt and its role in excluding the skeptic from the charmed circle of the believer's religion and its powers" (Gottlieb 1992:45).

Although Raúl is skeptical and does not use the mountain, he reflects a Salasacan theory of the mind and the role of faith in effecting pacts with the mountain. Various mental states affect a supplicant's ritual offerings to the mountain; Esteban also mentioned the role of faith in making the ritual work. Raúl and his brother mentioned faith, courage, and fear. Fear can cause one to become traumatized and trap one on the powerful mountain. There is a clear relationship between the mountain and the emotional state of the person who leaves an offering. When Raúl said that he doesn't use the sacred places, he nonetheless validated the beliefs of other people by saying that the places work for those who really believe. This attitude has significant implications for current anthropological concerns regarding individual meanings, the heterogeneity of cultures, and reflexivity on the part of the subjects of ethnographic investigations.

On several occasions I accompanied people to leave offerings at Quinchi Urcu. Marta, who narrated the story of the Quishuar tree (see chap. 2), is the mother of Carmenza. Both women have gone to pray and leave offerings at Cruz Pamba and Quinchi Urcu in order to improve their success in spinning wool and in breeding animals. Carmenza's daughter María also accompanied her grandmother and aunts to pray on Quinchi Urcu. Their stories show the experiences of three generations of women in the same family as they continue this local religious practice.

One day in 1992, Carmenza invited me to accompany her when she went to leave an offering in order to increase the number of animals she owned: "I want to clean out the guinea pig and rabbit cages and leave the excrement in Quinchi Urcu, but I have to do it on a Tuesday or Friday. If you clean the cages on a Tuesday or Friday and leave the droppings in Quinchi Urcu the animals will increase." Many Andeans, including the old shaman Manuel, perform rituals on Tuesdays or Fridays. These days were considered bad luck in Spanish lore, and an old saying holds that a marriage performed or a trip taken on a Tuesday or Friday would end badly. For many indigenous people, sacred time and space are not separated into "good" versus "evil." Rather, powerful saints, places, and days can be both beneficent and harmful. Another instance of this dual nature of power is the Quichua term *jambi*, which means both "medicine" and "poison." In the same way, the "bad omen" days of Spanish lore are good for healing rituals and offerings in Salasaca.

I went with Carmenza on the day she left the offering. At the crevice on the top of Quinchi Urcu we saw clothing, threads of all different colors, candles tied together in the form of a cross, and eggs. She explained that the eggs were from someone who underwent a cleansing to be healed, and that the eggs suck the sickness out of the body. But she wouldn't touch anything, in case someone had used them for witchcraft. There was also a bone with a white cloth tied around it. Carmenza explained:

> They made it *mayto* [swaddled]. They made a baby. When a child is sick, they have to dress up a bone or a guinea pig. The sick child sleeps hugging the doll, and while it's still dark outside two people go up to Quinchi Urcu and leave it here, in the middle of the Quinchi. When my nephew was a baby, he was very sick, and we did this for him, dressing up a guinea pig with colored ribbons. Now we want to do this for my brother's baby because he is very skinny. One should dress up a guinea pig and tie ribbons around its neck and body so that children don't get fright sickness.

Carmenza then pulled out a tuft of wool from her distaff and left it in the hole in order that she would spin faster.

On a separate occasion in 1997, when Carmenza was working at her job as a dishwasher in the city of Ambato, Marta went to Quinchi Urcu with her other daughters and son and with Carmenza's daughters, María, age thirteen at the time, and Leticia, age ten. One of Marta's daughters, Rosario, was pregnant. The women left spindles so that they would spin more, and they prayed for a safe and easy birth for Rosario. I interviewed María about her understanding of the offering. She and her aunts followed her grandmother's instructions for leaving the offering: "You know how Rosario is pregnant, right? We cleansed her stomach with a coin and placed it there, so that she wouldn't die this way, so that she would give birth easily. We said something like, 'help, help,' something like that, my grandmother said it. It must be God from above or who-knows-what [Qu. *imarí*] that helps. And she had an easy birth." María confirmed that leaving the little spindles and wool at the mountain shrine caused her to spin faster, but she didn't know how.

A woman in her thirties, Juliana, described Quinchi Urcu as a good place for healing sick children:

> In the plants on Quinchi Urcu, they send a guinea pig, and for a skinny child they make him sleep hugging a bone doll. At 4:00 in the

morning they leave it there. They go on *chiqi* [bad omen] Friday or chiqi Tuesday, so that the bad winds are out of the way. I have never done this, but my brother Juan did for his children. He left a guinea pig and a bone. . . . [Children get sick] from sleeping just anywhere. The rainbow follows them. They get diarrhea. By paying the mountain with a doll and a guinea pig, they fix the problem, the child gains weight. My brother did this for two of his children.

Palama, the mountain that is connected to Quinchi Urcu, has a large, cross-shaped crevice at the top called Nitón Cruz, where people also leave offerings. Marta described her experience with Nitón Cruz:

When I didn't have the urge to spin wool in order to make *bayetas* [women's shawls], I went with my companions from the Gallery [women's craft cooperative] to Nitón Cruz. We went, about five of us, to leave wool there. Now I spin. Some men cleanse their hands with coins or broken plates and leave them there in order to weave. After my friend cleansed her sheep and left a candle and wool in Nitón Cruz, the sheep gave birth to twins. I remember J. M [a musician who is now deceased] told me that he went to sleep on Nitón Cruz in order to play well. While sleeping there he met a person-like being [*runalaya*, *gentelaya*], but it wasn't a person. It must have been the Urcu Tayta [Mountain Father]. He taught J. M how to play, and just from that he began playing the violin very well. "I learned in my sleep," he said. It appeared in his eyes [*paibuj ñauhuipi ricurin*]. He went at 10 p.m. and returned at 5 a.m., knowing how to play.

Marta also took dirt from Nitón Cruz to put in the guinea pig cage. By taking dirt from this sacred place, she hoped to appropriate the power and energy of the mountain to help the guinea pigs grow and breed well. She added that pigs also breed and get fat if one cleanses them with a candle and leaves the candle with pig hair in Nitón Cruz. Her practice operates on the same principle as Sara's: cleansing the animal with a candle and leaving animal hairs in the mountain shrine results in the animal breeding. Just as taking a physical substance (hair, excrement) of an animal to the place will affect the animal, the dirt is considered to be part of the place; therefore, bringing the dirt into contact with the guinea pig cages will have a positive effect on the animals.

Cruz Pamba

Just as people's individual understandings of the powers of Quinchi Urcu are based partly on a collective body of narratives about the past rain-making ritual, some people refer to the body of narratives of those who had near-death experiences in their explanations of the powers of Cruz Pamba. Others associate it mainly with healing and animal fertility.

Emilia is Raúl's mother-in-law. An older, proud, matriarchal-type figure, she owns her house and the land where she and her husband live, and her grown married sons and grandsons also live on her land. Occasionally, when the family is drinking together during a fiesta, she will remind them that she is the owner of the land. Emilia raises bulls to rent out to mestizos for their town fiestas (Salasacan bulls are preferred for their perceived fierceness; see Cassagrande 1981). During most of my fieldwork Emilia was surrounded in her house by her children and grandchildren. By 2002, the houses were empty as children and grandchildren had migrated to the Galapagos Islands in search of construction work. One night, Emilia, now an elderly woman, visited Anita. As they sat by the fire, Emilia cried, "Why did they bother building a house on the land, or plowing their fields, just to leave them abandoned? Everyone is gone." Dollarization, economic pressures, and internal migration had severely transformed the household composition of this senior woman.

Emilia is knowledgeable in Salasacan history and traditions, and she explained the powers of Cruz Pamba to me: "Children get better and grow well after they are taken to Cruz Pamba, but someone other than the mother has to take them back; in order for it to work, a different person must carry the child home." Just as others reported that different roads should be taken to and from Cruz Pamba, different people should take the child there and bring it home, and the clothes must be put on in a different way (e.g., backwards) before returning home. These symbolic changes signify the ritual transformation that took place at Cruz Pamba.

Juliana told me of another use for Cruz Pamba: "Cruz Pamba is good for finding out who robbed you. With a candle you have to cleanse the place that the item was stolen from. After leaving the candle in Cruz Pamba, from one mouth to another, it will "come out" from someone's mouth [shimi shimi shuq shimimunda lluqshin]." This statement suggests that the place "works on" people to make them volunteer information.

Keith Basso (1984) reported an Apache narrative in which someone used witchcraft to work "with words" on a person's mind and make him say foolish things. Juliana's statement suggests that the place operates in a similar manner: it works on people to make them talk and make the information about the robbery "come out" of someone's mouth, just as it works on people's desires and "urges them" to spin wool.

Raúl, his younger brother, and his wife gave a more elaborate description that links Cruz Pamba with Ecuador's human geography and with the cauldron of the afterlife: "It's there all right, the cauldron. Those who have died and come back have seen it. In this place, there is a hole. Women who don't want to have children go alone at night, on the *chiqi puncha* ("bad omen" days: Tuesdays and Fridays)."

His wife interjected, "No, they go when the sun is very bright [*indi pala*] in the afternoon, just before it sets." Raúl continued:

> Oh. A woman who doesn't want to have children must go alone, but without looking when the mountain whistles in order to trick her. One must enter by way of [the road] Cruz Pamba Ñan and leave by [the road] Calli Ñan, but without looking back. There at Cruz Pamba, where the roads meet, she has to roll in the dirt and cry to God about how poor she is, how she has no land, and beg him not to give her any more children. While she is rolling the mountain tries to trick her, there in Cruz Pamba, where the cauldron is, close to the hole. The mountain Quinchi whistles. It's pure magic. But she is the only one who hears it. If she turns around to look, her act will be worthless.

Although the practice of crying at Cruz Pamba in order to prevent pregnancy is known, people today use contraceptives including injections, oral contraceptives, tubal ligation, and vasectomies.

I interviewed another married couple together. Gladys and Boris told me of their own understandings of sacred places. Gladys worked for some time as a dishwasher at the market in the city of Ambato. Boris weaves tapestries and sells them to his Otavalan compadre, who then sells them to foreign tourists. Boris and Gladys have three children. They had hoped that their eldest daughter would finish high school and study at the university, but she dropped out of school to work as a housekeeper and earn money. Their son migrated to France with Boris's brother, and he stayed there for some time. Their youngest daughter seems studious and might fulfill her parents' hopes of sending a child to the university.

In their discussion of sacred places, Gladys and Boris related Cruz Pamba to the fiesta of Caporales, in which Salasacan men perform dressed as Afro-Ecuadorian soldiers. They also referred to narratives of people who had near-death experiences. Near-death experiences are related to Caporales because people believe that the character of the Afro-Ecuadorian soldier exists in the afterlife to protect the fiesta sponsor from being "caught" in the cauldron by the devils. They also associate sacred places with the fiesta cycle, abundant food, and San Buenaventura:

> GLADYS: People go to Cruz Pamba, to ask God, they put money there to beg God to help us in something, to have luck we go there. The *negros* and doñas [characters in the festival of Caporales] go there. All fiestas go there [to dance]. They say it's *milagroso* [miraculous]. The souls go there, don't they? Don't they say there is a cauldron there? Or is that in the cemetery?
>
> BORIS: No, it's in Cruz Pamba, don't you know where that cross stands now, the one that the alcaldes placed there? You know, there's a road that goes here, a road that goes there, a road that goes to Pelileo, that's where the cauldron is. You know, where those that celebrate the fiesta of Caporales worship. Don't they get help in the fiesta?
>
> RC: Who helps?
>
> BORIS: The devil. It's *sagrado* [sacred], Cruz Pamba. There they ask God and he helps. Everything—corn, potatoes, grains, beans—he helps bring them [*apachan*]. Asking there, he helps in everything, God is there or the devil is there. Some people who sponsor the fiesta [of Caporales] leave grains there in the hole at the time of the fiesta, in order to produce more. They also go down to [the hamlet] Chilca-pamba. There is a saint there. In Cruz Pamba it's the same. They dance there, they drink.
>
> GLADYS: Just as I cleanse the animals [large animals] and leave a candle and plants in San Antonio Teligote, Cruz Pamba is the same. When the rabbits or guinea pigs are dying, I always cleanse them with a bundle of plants and leave it. For sick children, too, they leave the plants, after doing a cleansing. In order to make someone become healthy, cleansing and leaving it [the cleansing material] in Cruz

Pamba is good. Tuesdays and Fridays people do it. They take the child there, take off the shirt, and make [him or her] roll around on the ground. A sick child who doesn't want to sleep, they take him there and ask God, making the naked child roll around in the dirt. Then they put the child's clothes on inside out [*lluquisha*, reversed].

RC: How does it work?

GLADYS: It works! They do get better; doing this, they get better. Cruz Pamba helps [*jursayachin*; it makes one strong]. It's miraculous. We go to Cruz Pamba on Fridays and Saturdays, cleansing our guinea pigs. [We cleanse] rabbits and guinea pigs, cleansing them with plant bundles. We leave them on the ground. We leave them, praying for help. We say, "Please help the guinea pigs to grow; they don't want to breed [*catish*]," so that they breed. Some people leave guinea pig droppings. We take a sack full of *mancha yura, santamaría, rudan, tschindi, capus panga, uqsha, sigsig* [types of plants], we leave these. For other animals—the large ones like sheep, cows, and burros— I just cleanse with a candle and leave it in Teligote. I don't know why, but they have traditionally done it this way, guinea pigs, rabbits, and cleansing sick children [in Cruz Pamba]. When a child is sick with diarrhea, they rub [the child's body] with plants and leave them there, but not in this road but from another road one must enter, from Calli Ñan. Because they say that it's not good to go by this road [that one took arriving there], one must follow a different road [back].

Gladys uses Teligote for rituals concerning the health and fertility of large livestock, and Cruz Pamba for rituals concerning the health and fertility of small animals and to heal children. Like other interviewees, Gladys responded to my question about how the ritual offerings work by asserting simply that they *do* work. She used the Spanish word for "miraculous" to describe the power of the sacred crossroads. But the dual nature of the power at Cruz Pamba leads to ambivalence about who or what helps people who pray and worship there (through dancing during festivals). Gladys and her husband said it could be God or the devil.

Luis, the respected prayer-maker (see chap. 4) reported:

For instance, if one has a toothache, they should cleanse with a candle and leave it there [at Cruz Pamba], saying, "Please help." There it calms, but (only) upon believing with faith [*fein criiqi*], having faith [*feda charisha*]. There, indeed, are the most important roads, Cruz Pamba Ñan and Calli Ñan, which comes directly from Chilcapamba. That is an old, old, old, old road; since the time of our great-great-grandparents they have followed that road. It is the path that goes into the road to Pelileo. Then down from there is the *huasha* [back/east] *pugru* [depression], the one they call Cuchinilla Pugru. It's like a gorge, going down to the end of Salasaca. . . .

Luis, like others, emphasizes the importance of believing and having faith. He also emphasizes roads and stresses the *antiquity* of the road. Through the road Calli Ñan he links different places: the plaza of Chilcapamba, the depression called Cuchinilla Pugru, and the town of Pelileo. Cuchinilla Pugru is a place along the road to Pelileo where people say the good and bad souls reside (chap. 4). For Luis, the description of Cruz Pamba links it to other significant local places and ancient pathways.

This sample of individual experiences with a sacred mountain reveals the nuances of what a "sacred place" means in lived, embodied experience. The first three individuals, Sara, Julio, and Esteban, drew on the discourse of older generations—such as narratives about rain-making rituals and talented musicians—in order to make their decisions to use the mountain to assist with different goals. They each had very real experiences—fertile, reproductive animals; hair that grew; a spirit who appeared in a dream. Others report having their bodies healed after leaving an offering, or getting the urge to spin wool or weave. Several people referred to the visions of those who had near-death experiences. The experiences are embodied; thus, the interpretive community creates a field of religious experience that impinges on individual bodies and mental states. When they tell of their own experiences, they contribute to the discourse that maintains the sacrality and power of the mountain, adding their own narrative threads to the anecdotal evidence that is passed down through generations.

Conclusion

Sacred places are a fundamental part of cosmology throughout the Andes (Allen 1988; Bastien 1978; Sallnow 1987). In this chapter I presented Salasacan views about their own lived experiences with shared, historical, sacred places to show the exact nature of the relationship with the sacred landscape today. I began the chapter with an excerpt from a colonial document to give historical perspective to the practices described here. In the eighteenth century, natives of the northern Ecuadorian province of Imbabura gathered at a mountain shrine to pray for an end to a severe drought. The local priest used the doctrina, the obligatory gathering for Catholic religious instruction, to publicly punish one woman for participating in such "idolatry." Salasacans have their own memories of a similar gathering, in the twentieth century, at their mountain shrine on Quinchi Urcu. The Salasacan stories confirm the success of the offering and prayers: it subsequently rained.

Today, younger generations draw on this knowledge and continue the practices of leaving mountain offerings and praying to the mountain mother and to sacred crossroads. Some individuals who migrated to the United States, France, and Spain prayed and left offerings to the local mountain mother prior to their trips, seeking future international success. Furthermore, Salasacans continue the practices of guinea pig divination and using a shamanic network, all of which were discussed by the archbishop of Quito in his 1668 *Itinerario*. These individuals maintain lived religion through continuing practice. Such private acts are based on narrative histories and collective memories of the sacred places. People associate Catholic saints with sacred places, and they connect saints and sacred geography in a complex cosmology that is tied to the fiesta cycle, agriculture, and weaving. Thus, during specified times, Salasacans continuously perform collective rituals that traverse sacred pathways in order to express a shared identity and common heritage, and many anonymous individuals use the same sites on their own time, as they see fit.

The rituals and traditions I discussed throughout this book serve as markers of Salasacan identity. People are aware of the uniqueness of their customs and reflect on the meanings of local rituals to their own sense of identity as part of a unique indigenous culture in Ecuador. For example, more than one Salasacan spoke with pride about how migrants, both domestic and international, make great efforts to return to Salasaca for the Day of the Dead, November 2, to gather in the cemetery with their family members. As one woman stated, "On this day you have to reunite with your family, even if you are angry with them."

At the same time, there has been a sense for years that some of the traditions, such as fiestas and expensive funerals, are not practical in today's world. The land base in the Andes is shrinking, with plots being divided into smaller and smaller portions with each generation of children. The cost of living is rising, and many families want their children to get university educations. Wages in Ecuador are low, and few jobs are available in the cities around Salasaca. Salasacan men have been migrating for generations, often working for months at a time on coastal plantations or at construction jobs in the Galapagos and elsewhere. Today, many of their wives and children are following them, leaving houses and fields abandoned. Going into debt to feed the whole community in honor of a saint's feast day seems inappropriate to some. One man told me, "I'd rather spend money on my children's education than on a fiesta." Another man suggested that the old fiestas were going to die out, "But that's O.K.," he said, "they will be replaced by other types of celebrations, such as folkloric musical performances." Although over the years some people have predicted to me that the fiestas would die out, others are making efforts to keep them going.

As I have argued in this book, Salasacans have always been active in shaping their own religious history. Although indigenous people were forced to convert to Catholicism, colonial evangelization projects resulted in new forms of indigenous memory: festival sponsors express Salasacan identity as one of people with ties to the land and a shared past through Andean placemaking ceremonies; Catholic prayers have been re-centered in a Quichua oratory that focuses on the teachings of the ancestors, and the Catholic feast day of Corpus Christi is a context for performing genealogical memory. In addition to these rituals, Peter Wogan (2004) has shown how Salasacans have appropriated church literacy practices as a means of commemorating their antecessors. The ceremonial blessings of the santa mesa, based on Catholic prayers that were forced on indigenous people during the colonial period, are a verbal art linking the Catholic God to local agricultural practices, native foods, the Earth Mother, and sami. Such prayers are now indigenous tradition: they serve to remind people of their collective past and common heritage.

Although there certainly was domination and indigenous resistance during Catholic evangelization efforts, there was also engagement and

FIGURE 8.3. A Salasacan man and woman walk from Quinchi Urcu to Palama.

negotiation (see Abercrombie 1998b; Dover 1992). There were negotiations over the quishuar tree and sponsorship appointments, and compromises among priests, vicars, indigenous governors, and festival sponsors. The rituals that people developed from these religious encounters emphasize a sense of indigenous collective identity. Through participation in these collective rituals, and through multiple, individual, private acts, Salasacans sustain and continuously re-create their religion.

Notes

Chapter 1: The Salasca Runa

1. Attempts to define religion have led to contentious discussions that are beyond the scope of this book. I will rely on Edward B. Tylor's definition of religion as "belief in spiritual beings" (Tylor 1965:11). Spiritual beings in this context include God, the devil, saints, souls, mountain spirits, and spirit masters of pathways and springs.

2. I found some colonial documents following a reference in Carrera Colin (1981). There is no mention of Salasaca as a place or a people in the writings of colonial chroniclers. It is not mentioned among the eighteen towns in the Ambato region that were settled (*reducidos*) by Antonio de Clavijo in 1584. Neither Juan de Velasco's *Historia del Reino de Quito* (1998 [1788]) nor any of the reports contained in the *Relaciones histórico-geográficas de la Audiencia de Quito* (Ponce Leiva 1991) mention Salasaca. In his 1771 *Descripción histórico-topográfica de la provincia de Quito* the Jesuit priest Mario Cicala did mention Salasaca as an annex of the town of Pelileo: "In its district [Pelileo] has various annexes of Salasaca Indians with little churches or chapels such as Llumaqui, Panchanlica, Guambaló, San Ildefonso, etc., by which the priest has in his charge around 900 souls" (Cicala 1994 [1771]:392).

The area Cicala mentions is much more extensive than the modernday boundaries of Salasaca, and he seems to be subsuming various indigenous populations under the term "Salasaca Indians."

3. The current estimate of the Salasacan population is twelve thousand, whereas estimates for the Saraguros number around twenty-two thousand (www.saraguro.org). The area of Salasaca today is approximately fourteen square kilometers (Carrasco A. 1982:21).

4. I use the term *blanco-mestizo* to refer to Ecuadorian whites and people of mixed heritage. Salasacans use the term *cholos* to refer collectively to Spanish-speaking Ecuadorians who do not wear indigenous ethnic attire. In Salasacan usage cholos is a complicated term that can also be translated as "whites" (see Weismantel 2001). I use *chola* here to refer to the non-Salasacan market women who come to the community to sell food.

5. See Rappaport (1994, 1998). In his analysis of indigenous religion in colonial Mexico, William Taylor (1996) emphasizes the importance of studying local religion and the role of individual priests. In order to understand rituals of the Bolivian Aymara, Thomas Abercrombie (1998b) combined extensive archival research with ethnographic fieldwork to show how rituals are a form of Andean memory. Peter Wogan's book *Magical Writing in Salasaca* (2004) is the first study of Salasacan rituals to focus on indigenous responses to church and state policies. Barry Lyons' 2006 book *Remembering the Hacienda* also

combines archival research with ethnography and oral histories of indigenous people in Chimborazo Province, Ecuador. Although my research is based mainly on participant-observation and ethnographic interviews, I also make use of oral histories and archival documents, but the archival materials on Salasaca are scant. I could not find any church documents from either the colonial period or the early nation-building years.

6. Barbara Tedlock's distinction between memoirs and narrative ethnographies is useful here. "In contrast to memoirs, narrative ethnographies focus not on the ethnographer herself, but rather on the character and process of the ethnographic dialogue or encounter" (1991:78). A narrative ethnography presents not only the author's experiences, but also ethnographic data and cultural analysis. Also, whereas the anthropologist is the main character in a memoir, in an ethnographic narrative the anthropologist is a secondary character.

Chapter 3: Textual Strategies and Ritual Control in Early Twentieth-Century Salasaca

1. Salasacan cargo holders are exclusively male, but among the Saraguros of the southern Ecuadorian Andes, women serve as festival sponsors in their own right, independently of their husbands. This may be a continuation of the Andean value of gender parallelism (Belote and Belote 1989).

2. Note that the grandfather's last name was Masaquiza, and the petitioners' last names were Jerez and Anancolla. By this time, civil authorities were recording indigenous people using the father's last name, which suggests that these petitioners were claiming inheritance from their mother's father. This is not certain, however, since we do not know how Salasacans were transmitting last names at this time, nor do we know whether civil authorities correctly recorded people's last names.

Chapter 4: Prayer and Placemaking in the Andes

1. Ideally, an alcalde should serve for two years, but the two years do not have to be served consecutively. A man who has served only one year is referred to as *chulla*, "missing the other half." One man was pressured by friends to finish up his service twenty years after his first year as alcalde. His friends began calling him a dog for not sponsoring the fiestas for a second year. So, as an old man, he undertook the sponsorship position again.

2. Such local manifestations of Catholic icons are not unique to Salasacans, or even to Latin Americans. European Catholic peasants also reported miraculous appearances of saints and crucifixes at local places on the landscape, evoking a tension between the institutional church and local religion (Christian 1981; L. Taylor 1995). Writing of local religion in sixteenth-century Spain, William Christian (1981) views the localization of sacred powers in rural landscapes as a resistance to central church power. Lawrence Taylor (1995) makes a similar argument for the sacred wells of rural Ireland. Certainly the localization of the sacred can be seen as an appropriation of powers controlled by the church. Salasacans, however, do not view their practices as a form of resistance to church power. When they fled to the mountain shrine on Quinchi Urcu after the earthquake, it was not

because they rejected the church but because they turned to a time-honored practice that had worked for them in the past. While Salasacans might criticize individual clergy members, they are also dependent on the clergy to administer the sacraments that mark important rites of passage in their lives.

3. Native North Andean chiefs could mobilize labor to work their maize fields and redistribute maize to their subjects in the form of beer on festive occasions (Salomon 1986:81). Throughout the time of my fieldwork, the alcaldes were required to produce large amounts of maize beer for sharing.

4. Salasacan elders recall a time when the community was divided into two sides that would engage in battles (called *tutunis*) between the men, women, and youths of each side. Someone would round up people by blowing on a conch shell or bull horn, and sometimes there would be a drummer and maize beer to accompany the battles. These fights ended when one man had his tooth knocked out and took legal action to have the fights banned in his community. During the time of my fieldwork in 1997–98, some adults expressed interest in recording oral histories about who the "really strong" fighters were in the past.

5. When I asked Luis why people cried more for the female bread baby, he said "because for us the dear little female is more significant." In practice, however, Salasacans do not prefer female children per se, but rather a balance of male and female children.

Chapter 5: Life Lessons at a Time of Death

1. For descriptions and analysis of the huayru and similar dice games in Ecuador see Brownrigg 1989; Karsten 1930, 1935; Ulloa 1772:407–8; and N. Whitten 1976. For descriptions pertaining to other parts of South America, see Carter 1968; Cooper 1963; Gentile 1998; and Harris 1982. Frank Salomon (2002) describes a divination game called *huayrona* in Huarochirí, Peru. This game is not played during funerals but at the change of political authorities during the New Year.

2. A significant road in Salasaca is the road called Calli Ñan, which connects old Salasaca, now called Chilcapamba, to the local center of church and state authority in Pelileo. The ancient trail has a spirit master, a "dueño" called Tayta Calli Ñan. Older Salasacans say that when walking alone at night one should call out his name, "Tayta Calli Ñan!" to make him disappear. Not only do roads have spirit masters, but phantom roads can appear to lead a drunk or otherwise unhealthy man down the wrong path. As with weddings, funerals, and festivals, movement along particular roads is a fundamental part of ritual offerings for good health. If one goes to leave medicinal plants or an offering for an ill person at Cruz Pamba, one must take one road to the shrine, return on the other road, and never turn around to look back. If this procedure is not followed, the rite will fail.

Chapter 6: Tales of Amazonia

1. This hallucinogenic brew is made from a vine (one of three species of *Banisteriopsis*) mixed with other plants. A few elderly Salasacans told of drinking the brew, in consultation with lowland shamans, in order to see who had robbed them.

2. The Shuar boycotted the 1992 March for Land and Life (Norm Whitten, personal communication). Perhaps the shaman was actually Achuar or Shiwiar, since Carlos could not remember exactly where he was from.

Chapter 7: Shamanism

1. Although they consider themselves socially, racially, and culturally superior to "indios," these small-town blanco-mestizos are considered unsophisticated by urban elites (see Weismantel 2001:48).

References Cited

Archives

Archivo Arzobispal de Quito (AAQ)
Archivo General de Indias, Seville (AGI/S)
Archivo Histórico de la Curia de Ambato (ACA)
Archivo Nacional del Ecuador (ANE; followed by series: Cazicazgos, Indígenas, or Encomiendas)

References

AGI/S, Quito, 13, R.13, N38
1666–11–15 Estado de la encomienda de Pelileo y agravios a sus indios. http://pares .mcu.es.

ANE Cazicazgos (Caz.)
1-I-1728 Don Francisco Ati Haja, cacique principal y governador de los pueblos de Sigchos, Isinliví, y Toacazo, trae demanda sobre unos indios de la familia y apellido Masaquisas.

ANE Indígenas (Ind.)
15-II-1712 Don Francisco Machaquicha, cacique principal de San Buena Ventura de Salasaca, pide Real provisión para no repartir entero a sus vecinos.
9-III-1743 Carlos Masaquisa, indio natural del pueblo de Pelileo, pide no estar obligado de servir en el obraje de Sn. Ildefonso por no ser de la comunidad.

Abercrombie, Thomas
1998a Commentary. *Journal of Latin American Anthropology* 3(3):150–67.
1998b *Pathways of Memory and Power.* Madison: University of Wisconsin Press.

Abu-Lughod, Lila
1991 Writing against Culture. In *Recapturing Anthropology: Working in the Present,* ed. Richard G. Fox, 137–62. Santa Fe, N.M.: School of American Research Press.

Adams, Richard Newbold
1975 *Energy and Structure: A Theory of Social Power.* Austin: University of Texas Press.

Albornoz, Oswaldo
1963 *Historia de la acción clerical en el Ecuador: Desde la conquista hasta nuestros días.* Quito: Ediciones Soltierra.

Allen, Catherine J.

1988   *The Hold Life Has: Coca and Cultural Identity in an Andean Community.* Washington, D.C.: Smithsonian Institution Press.

"Autos de visitas pastorales." San Pedro de Pelileo, Ecuador: Casa Parroquial.

Babcock, Barbara

1996   Arrange Me into Disorder: Fragments and Reflections on Ritual Clowning. In *Readings in Ritual Studies*, ed. Ronald L. Grimes, 1–21. Upper Saddle River, N.J.: Prentice Hall.

Bacigalupo, Ana Mariella

2007   *Shamans of the Foye Tree: Gender, Power, and Healing among the Chilean Mapuche.* Austin: University of Texas Press.

Barnes, Monica

1992   Catechisms and Confessionarios: Distorting Mirrors of Andean Societies. In *Andean Cosmologies through Time*, ed. Robert V. H. Dover, Katharine E. Seibold, and John H. McDowell, 67–94. Bloomington: Indiana University Press.

Barreno a González Suárez

1907   Luis Octavio Barreno a González Suárez pide obsequie para Salasaca imagen de la Virgen y 2 crucifijos. Jan. 8, Legajos IV, ACA.

Basso, Keith H.

1984   "Stalking with Stories": Names, Places, and Moral Narratives among the Western Apache. In *Text, Play, and Story: The Construction and Reconstruction of Self and Society*, ed. Edward M. Bruner, 19–55. Prospect Heights, Ill.: Waveland.

Bastien, Joseph

1978   *Mountain of the Condor: Metaphor and Ritual in an Andean Ayllu.* St. Paul, Minn.: West Publishing Co.

Bauman, Richard

1984   *Verbal Art as Performance.* Prospect Heights, Ill.: Waveland.

Bauman, Richard, and Charles Briggs

1990   Poetics and Performance as Critical Perspectives on Language and Social Life. *Annual Review of Anthropology* 19:59–88.

Belote, Linda, and Jim Belote

1989   Gender, Ethnicity, and Modernization: Saraguro Women in a Changing World. In *Multidisciplinary Studies in Andean Anthropology*, ed. Virginia J. Vitzthum, 101–17. Michigan Discussions in Anthropology 8. Ann Arbor: University of Michigan.

Bourdieu, Pierre

1990   *In Other Words: Essays towards a Reflexive Sociology.* Stanford, Calif.: Stanford University Press.

Brownrigg, Leslie Ann

1977   Variaciones del parentesco Cañari. In *Temas sobre la continuidad y adaptación cultural ecuatoriana*, ed. Marcelo F. Naranjo, José L. Pereira V., and Norman E. Whitten Jr., 25–44. Quito: PUCE.

1989   Juego de pishca al huairu en Quingeo, Azuay. *Revista de Antropología.* [Casa de la Cultura Ecuatoriana–Núcleo del Azuay] 10:9–38.

Burger, Richard L.

1992   *Chavin and the Origins of the Andean Civilization.* New York: Thames and Hudson.

Butler, Barbara Y.

2006   *Holy Intoxication to Drunken Dissipation: Alcohol among Quichua Speakers in Otavalo, Ecuador.* Albuquerque: University of New Mexico Press.

Caizabanda al Arzobispo

1908   Manuel Caizabanda Gobernador de Salasaca al Arzobispo de Quito. May 1908, Legajos IV, ACA.

Calderón, Eduardo, Richard Cowan, Douglas Sharon, and F. Kaye Sharon

1999   *Eduardo el Curandero: The Words of a Peruvian Healer.* Berkeley: North Atlantic Books.

Carrasco A., Eulalia

1982   *Salasaca: la organización social y el alcalde.* Quito: Mundo Andino.

Carrera Colin, Juan

1981   Apuntes para una investigación etnohistórica de los casicazgos. *Cultura* 4(11):129–79. (Quito: Banco Central de Ecuador.)

Carrillo a Subsecretario

1908   Carrillo a Subsecretario Pablo Sánchez: Da cuenta respecto a alcaldes de Salasaca. Oct. 17. Legajos IV, ACA.

Carter, William E.

1968   Secular Reinforcement in Aymara Death Ritual. *American Anthropologist* 70:238–63.

Casey, Edward S.

1996   How to Get from Space to Place in a Fairly Short Stretch of Time. In *Senses of Place*, ed. Steven Feld and Keith H. Basso, 13–52. Santa Fe, N.M.: School of American Research.

Cassagrande, Joseph B.

1981   Strategies for Survival: The Indians of Highland Ecuador. In *Cultural Transformations and Ethnicity in Modern Ecuador*, ed. Norman E. Whitten Jr., 260–77. Urbana and Chicago: University of Illinois Press.

Chango, María, and Agustín Jerez
1995   Reis Pishta. In *La fiesta religiosa indígena en el Ecuador*, ed. Luz del Alba Moya, 115–30. Quito: Abya-Yala.

Chango al Arzobispo
1914   Raimundo Chango, Gobernador de Salasaca envía nombres para los empleados del caserío. Dec. 18, Legajos IV, ACA.

Christian, William A., Jr.
1981   *Local Religion in Sixteenth-Century Spain.* Princeton: Princeton University Press.

Cicala, Mario
1994 [1771]   *Descripción histórico-topográfica de la provincia de Quito de la Compañía de Jesús.* Quito: Biblioteca Ecuatoriana "Aurelio Espinosa Pólit."

Cobo, Bernabé, and Roland Hamilton
1990   *Inca Religion and Customs.* Austin: University of Texas Press.

Colloredo-Mansfeld, Rudi
2003   Tigua Migrant Communities and the Possibilities for Autonomy among Urban *Indígenas*. In *Millennial Ecuador: Critical Essays on Cultural Transformations and Social Dynamics*, ed. Norman E. Whitten Jr., 275–95. Iowa City: University of Iowa Press.

CONAIE
1997   *Proyecto político de la CONAIE.* Quito: Ibis-Dinamarca.

Connerton, Paul
1989   *How Societies Remember.* Cambridge and New York: Cambridge University Press.

Cooper, John M.
1963   Games and Gambling. In *Handbook of South American Indians.* Vol. 5, *The Comparative Ethnology of South American Indians*, ed. Julian Steward, 503–24. New York: Cooper Square.

Corr, Rachel
2002   Reciprocity, Communion, and Sacrifice: Food in Andean Ritual and Social Life. *Food and Foodways* 10:1–25.
2003a The Catholic Church, Ritual, and Power in Salasaca. In *Millennial Ecuador: Critical Essays on Cultural Transformations and Social Dynamics*, ed. Norman E. Whitten Jr., 102–28. Iowa City: University of Iowa Press.
2003b Ritual, Knowledge, and the Politics of Identity in Andean Festivities. *Ethnology* 42(1):39–54
2004   To Throw the Blessing: Poetics, Prayer, and Performance in the Andes. *Journal of Latin American Anthropology* 9(2):382–408.
2008   Death, Dice, and Divination: Rethinking Religion and Play in South America. *Journal of Latin American and Caribbean Anthropology* 13(1):2–21.

Cuato a Arzobispo
1908   Remigio Cuato a Arzobispo: Agustín Masaquiza ha sido nombrado alcalde mayor. Oct. 17. Legajos IV, ACA.

Dean, Carolyn

1999 *Inka Bodies and the Body of Christ: Corpus Christi in Colonial Cuzco, Peru.* Durham, N.C., and London: Duke University Press.

De la Torre, Carlos María

1907a Informe detallado sobre la parroquia de Pelileo. Jan. 23. Legajos IV, ACA.

1907b Carlos María de la Torre al Arzobispo sobre la imagen de la Santísima Virgen obsequiada a los indígenas de Salasaca. Jan. 29. Legajos IV, ACA.

Dougherty, Janet W. D., and James Fernandez

1981 Introduction to Symbolism and Cognition. Special issue, *American Ethnologist* 8(3):413–21.

Dover, Robert V. H.

1992 Introduction to *Andean Cosmologies through Time: Persistence and Emergence,* ed. Robert V. H. Dover, Katharine E. Seibold, and John H. McDowell, 1–16. Bloomington: Indiana University Press.

Drewal, Margaret Thompson

1992 *Yoruba Ritual: Performers, Play, Agency.* Bloomington: Indiana University Press.

Feld, Steven, and Keith H. Basso, eds.

1996 *Senses of Place.* Santa Fe, N.M.: School of American Research Press.

Ferán al Vicario General

1910 Luis L. Ferán al Vicario: Informa sobre doctrinas de indios sobre coadjutores. Nov. 11, Legajos IV, ACA.

Fernandez, James

1965 Symbolic Consensus in a Fang Reformative Cult. *American Anthropologist* 67:902–29.

Firth, Raymond William

1973 *Symbols: Public and Private.* Ithaca, N.Y.: Cornell University Press.

Foster, George

1960 *Culture and Conquest: America's Spanish Heritage.* New York: Wenner-Gren Foundation for Anthropological Research.

Geertz, Clifford

1973 *The Interpretation of Cultures.* New York: Basic Books.

Gentile L., Margarita E.

1998 La Pichca: oráculo y juego de fortuna (su persistencia en el espacio y tiempo andinos). *Bulletin de l'Institut Français d'Études Andines* 27(1):75–131.

Gillespie, Susan D.

1993 Power, Pathways, and Appropriations in Mesoamerican Art. In *Imagery and Creativity: Ethnoaesthetics and Art Worlds in the Americas,* ed. Dorothea S. Whitten and Norman E. Whitten Jr., 67–107. Tucson: University of Arizona Press.

Glass-Coffin, Bonnie

1998   *The Gift of Life: Female Spirituality and Healing in Northern Peru.* Albuquerque: University of New Mexico Press.

Gottlieb, Alma

1992   *Under the Kapok Tree: Identity and Difference in Beng Thought.* Bloomington: Indiana University Press.

Griffiths, Nicholas

1999   Introduction to *Spiritual Encounters*, ed. Nicolas Griffiths and Fernando Cervantes, 1–42. Lincoln: University of Nebraska Press.

Guerrero, Andrés

1997   The Construction of a Ventriloquist's Image: Liberal Discourse and the 'Miserable Indian Race' in Late 19th-Century Ecuador. *Journal of Latin American Studies* 29:555–90.

2003   The Administration of Dominated Populations under a Regime of Customary Citizenship: The Case of Ecuador. In *After Spanish Rule: Postcolonial Predicaments of the Americas*, ed. Mark Thurner and Andrés Guerrero, 272–309. Durham, N.C.: Duke University Press.

Hamerly, Michael T.

2000   *Historical Bibliography of Ecuador.* Vol. 2, *Church History.* www.ecuatorianistas.org/bibliographies/hamerly/ecubib2c.html.

Harris, Olivia

1982   The Dead and the Devils among the Bolivian Laymi. In *Death and the Regeneration of Life*, ed. Maurice Bloch and Jonathan Parry, 45–73. New York: Cambridge University Press.

Harrison, Regina

1989   *Signs, Songs, and Memory in the Andes.* Austin: University of Texas Press.

Harvey, Penelope

1997   Peruvian Independence Day: Ritual, Memory, and the Erasure of Narrative. In *Creating Context in Andean Cultures*, ed. Rosaleen Howard-Malverde, 21–44. New York and Oxford: Oxford University Press.

Helms, Mary

1988   *Ulysses' Sail.* Princeton, N.J.: Princeton University Press.

Hill, Jonathan D.

1996   Introduction: Ethnogenesis in the Americas, 1492–1992. In *History, Power, and Identity: Ethnogenesis in the Americas, 1492–1992*, ed. Jonathan D. Hill, 1–19. Iowa City: University of Iowa Press.

Hirsch, Eric

1995   Landscape: Between Place and Space. In *The Anthropology of Landscape: Perspectives on Place and Space*, ed. Eric Hirsch and Michael O'Hanlon, 1–30. New York: Oxford University Press.

Hirsch, Eric, and Michael O'Hanlon, eds.

1995 *The Anthropology of Landscape: Perspectives on Place and Space.* New York: Oxford University Press.

Howard, Rosaleen

2002 Spinning a Yarn: Landscape, Memory, and Discourse Structure in Quechua Narratives. In *Narrative Threads: Accounting and Recounting in Andean Khipu*, ed. Jeffrey Quilter and Gary Urton, 26–49. Austin: University of Texas Press.

Huizinga, Johan

1955 *Homo Ludens: A Study of the Play-element in Culture.* Boston: Beacon Press.

Icaza, Jorge

1964 [1934] *Huasipungo. The Villagers, a Novel.* Carbondale: Southern Illinois University Press.

Isbell, Billie-Jean

1985 *To Defend Ourselves: Ecology and Ritual in an Andean Village.* Prospect Heights, Ill.: Waveland.

Jerez and Anancolla al Arzobispo

1913 José y Gerónimo Jerez e Ignacio Anancolla al ilustrísimo señor Arzobispo del Dióce-sis "sobre el cargo de Pindonero." May 17, Legajos IV, ACA.

Jerez Caisabanda, Carmen

2001 "No sé, las mujeres salasacas tenemos miedo a participar": Participación de la mujer salasaca en el ámbito comunal, organización y la educación intercultural bilingüe de Tungurahua. Master's thesis, Universidad Mayor de San Simón Cochabamba, Bolivia.

Kan, Sergei

1989 *Symbolic Immortality: The Tlingit Potlatch of the Nineteenth Century.* Washington, D.C.: Smithsonian Institution Press.

Karsten, Rafael

1930 *Ceremonial Games of the South American Indians.* Commentationes Humanarum Litterarum 3, no. 2. Helsinki: Societas Scientiarum Fenica.

1935 *The Head-hunters of Western Amazonas: The Life and Culture of the Jibaro Indians of Eastern Ecuador and Peru.* Commentationes Humanarum Litterarum 2, no. 1. Helsinki: Societas Scientiarum Fenica.

Lambert, Bernd

1977 Bilaterality in the Andes. In *Andean Kinship and Marriage*, ed. Ralph Bolton and Enrique Mayer, 1–27. Washington, D.C.: American Anthropological Association.

Lane, Kris

2003 Haunting the Present: Five Colonial Legacies for the New Millennium. In *Millennial Ecuador: Critical Essays on Cultural Transformations and Social Dynamics*, ed. Norman E. Whitten Jr., 75–101. Iowa City: University of Iowa Press.

Lara, Jorge S., ed.

2001 *Historia de la iglesia Católica en el Ecuador.* Vols. 1–3. Quito: Ediciones Abya-Yala.

Lathrap, Donald W.

1985 Jaws: The Control of Power in the Early Nuclear American Ceremonial Center. In *Early Ceremonial Architecture in the Andes,* ed. Christopher B. Donnan, 241–62. Washington, D.C.: Dumbarton Oaks.

Le Goff, Jacques

1984 *The Birth of Purgatory.* Chicago: University of Chicago Press.

Lévi-Strauss, Claude

1985 [1963] The Sorcerer and His Magic. In *Magic, Witchcraft, and Religion: An Anthropological Study of the Supernatural,* ed. Arthur C. Lehmann and James E. Myers, 263–72. Palo Alto: Mayfield.

Lewis, Ioan M.

1971 *Ecstatic Religion: An Anthropological Study of Spirit Possession and Shamanism.* Harmondsworth, U.K.: Penguin.

Lyons, Barry J.

2006 *Remembering the Hacienda: Religion, Authority, and Social Change in Highland Ecuador.* Austin: University of Texas Press.

MacCormack, Sabine

1991 *Religion in the Andes.* Princeton, N.J.: Princeton University Press.

Mannheim, Bruce

1991 *The Language of the Inca since the European Invasion.* Austin: University of Texas Press.

Mannheim, Bruce, and Dennis Tedlock, eds.

1995 Introduction to *The Dialogic Emergence of Culture,* 1–32. Urbana and Chicago: University of Illinois Press.

Mannheim, Bruce, and Krista Van Vleet

1998 The Dialogics of Southern Quechua Narrative. *American Anthropologist* 100(2):326–46.

Masaquiza a Arzobispo

1908 Cecilio Masaquiza a Arzobispo pide se nombre alcalde de doctrina. Oct. 22, Legajos IV, ACA.

Masaquiza, Jeres, Pilla, and Jiménes al Imo. Señor

1885 Silverio Masaquiza, Bernardo Jeres, Agustín Pilla y Félix Jiménes al Imo. Señor. AAQ.

Masaquiza Masaquiza, José

1995 Los Salasacas. In *Identidades indias en el Ecuador contemporáneo,* ed. José Almeida Vinueza, 213–46. Cayambe, Ecuador: Ediciones Abya-Yala.

Mayer, Enrique

1977 Beyond the Nuclear Family. In *Andean Kinship and Marriage*, ed. Ralph Bolton and Enrique Mayer, 60–80. Washington, D.C.: American Anthropological Association.

McDowell, John Holmes

2000 Collaborative Ethnopoetics: A View from the Sibundoy Valley. In *Translating Native Latin American Verbal Art*, ed. Kay Sammons and Joel Sherzer, 211–32. Washington, D.C.: Smithsonian Institution Press.

Melo a Vicario General

1885 Vicente Melo al Imo. Sr. Vicario General de la Arquidiócesis. Pelileo, April 4, AAQ.

Miller, David LeRoy

1970 *Gods and Games: Toward a Theology of Play.* New York: World.

Miller, Laura

1998 Salasaca. In *Costume and Identity in Highland Ecuador*, ed. Ann Pollard Rowe, 126–44. Seattle: University of Washington Press.

Mintz, Sidney W., and Eric R. Wolf

1950 An Analysis of Ritual Co-Parenthood (*Compadrazgo*). *Southwestern Journal of Anthropology* 6(4):341–68.

Miranda Torres, Carlos

1994 *Monseñor Vicente Cisneros Duran: ensayo biográfico.* Ambato, Ecuador: Valverde Editores.

Moreno Yánez, Segundo

1991 Los doctrineros "Wiracochas" recreadores de nuevas formas culturales. In *Reproducción y transformación de las sociedades andinas, siglos XVI–XX*, ed. Segundo Moreno Yánez and Frank Salomon, 529–53. Quito: Abya-Yala.

Moya, Ruth

1981 *Simbolismo y ritual en el Ecuador andino: el quichua en el español de Quito.* Otavalo, Ecuador: Instituto Otavaleño de Antropología.

Myerhoff, Barbara

1990 A Death in Due Time: The Construction of Self and Culture in Ritual Drama. *In Customs in Conflict: The Anthropology of a Changing World*, ed. Frank Manning and Jean-Marc Philibert, 87–121. Ontario: Broadview Press.

Navas de Pozo, Yolanda

1990 *Angamarca en el siglo XVI.* Quito: Abya-Yala.

Newson, Linda A.

1995 *Life and Death in Early Colonial Quito.* Norman: University of Oklahoma Press.

O'Connor, Erin

2007 *Gender, Indian, Nation: The Contradictions of Making Ecuador, 1830–1925.* Tucson: University of Arizona Press.

Orsi, Robert A.

2002 *The Madonna of 115th Street: Faith and Community in Italian Harlem, 1880–1950.* New Haven, Conn.: Yale University Press.

Orta, Andrew

1999 Syncretic Subjects and Body Politics: Doubleness, Personhood, and Aymara Catechists. *American Ethnologist* 26(4):864–89.

2004 *Catechizing Culture: Missionaries, Aymara, and the "New Evangelization."* New York: Columbia University Press.

Parsons, Elsie Worthington Clews

1945 *Peguche, Canton of Otavalo, Province of Imbabura, Ecuador: A Study of Andean Indians.* Chicago: University of Chicago Press.

Peñaherrera de Costales, Pieded, and Alfredo Costales Samaniego

1959 *Los Salasacas: investigación y elaboración.* Vol. 8. Quito: Instituto Ecuatoriano de Antropología.

Peña Montenegro, Alonso de la

1995 [1668] *Itinerario para párrocos de indios.* Ed. C. Beciero, M. Corrales, J. M. García Anoveros, and F. Maseda. 2 vols. Madrid: Consejo Superior de Investigaciones Científicas.

Ponce Leiva, Pilar

1991 *Relaciones histórico-geográficas de la Audiencia de Quito, S. XVI–XIX.* Vols. 1 and 2. Madrid: Consejo Superior de Investigaciones Científicas.

Powers, Karen Vieira

1995 *Andean Journeys: Migration, Ethnogenesis, and the State in Colonial Quito.* Albuquerque: University of New Mexico Press.

Pratt, Mary Louise

1992 *Imperial Eyes: Travel Writing and Transculturation.* London: Routledge.

Price, Richard

1965 Trial Marriage in the Andes. *Ethnology* 4(3):310–22.

Quishpe B., Jorge Marcelo

1999 *Transformación y reproducción indígena en los Andes septentrionales.* Quito: Abya-Yala.

Radcliffe, Sarah A.

1990 Marking the Boundaries between the Community, the State, and History in the Andes. *Journal of Latin American Studies* 22(3):575–94.

Radcliffe, Sarah A., and Sallie Westwood

1996 *Remaking the Nation: Place, Identity, and Politics in Latin America.* London: Routledge.

Rahier, Jean Muteba
1998 Blackness, the Racial/Spatial Order, Migrations, and Miss Ecuador 1995–96. *American Anthropologist* 100(2):421–30.

Rappaport, Joanne
1994 *Cumbe Reborn: An Andean Ethnography of History.* Chicago: University of Chicago Press.
1998 *The Politics of Memory: Native Historical Interpretation in the Colombian Andes.* Durham, N.C.: Duke University Press.

Rasnake, Roger
1986 Carnaval in Yura: Ritual Reflections on *Ayllu* and State Relations. *American Ethnologist* 13(4):662–80.

Relph, E. C.
1976 *Place and Placelessness.* London: Pion.

Rosaldo, Renato
1989 *Culture and Truth: The Remaking of Social Analysis.* Boston: Beacon Press.

Rowe, Ann Pollard, ed.
1998 *Costume and Identity in Highland Ecuador.* Seattle: University of Washington Press.

Rubin, Miri
1991 *Corpus Christi: The Eucharist in Late Medieval Culture.* Cambridge and New York: Cambridge University Press.

Sallnow, Michael J.
1987 *Pilgrims of the Andes: Regional Cults in Cusco.* Washington, D.C.: Smithsonian Institution Press.

Salomon, Frank
1981 Killing the Yumbo: A Ritual Drama of Northern Quito. In *Cultural Transformations and Ethnicity in Modern Ecuador,* ed. Norman E. Whitten Jr., 162–208. Urbana: University of Illinois Press.
1983 Shamanism and Politics in Late-Colonial Ecuador. *American Ethnologist* 10(3):413–28.
1986 *Native Lords of Quito in the Age of the Incas: The Political Economy of North-Andean Chiefdoms.* Cambridge and New York: Cambridge University Press.
1995 "The Beautiful Grandparents": Andean Ancestor Shrines and Mortuary Ritual as Seen through Colonial Records. In *Tombs for the Living: Andean Mortuary Practices,* ed. Tom D. Dillehay, 247–81. Washington, D.C.: Dumbarton Oaks.
2002 "¡Huayra huayra pichcamanta!": Augurio, risa, y regeneración en la política tradicional. *Bulletin de l'Institut Français d'Études Andines.* 31(1):1–22.

Salomon, Frank, and George L. Urioste
1991 *The Huarochiri Manuscript.* Austin: University of Texas Press.

Sánchez, J. V.

1908 Subsecretario a Carrillo: Pide indicar a cuales de 2 candidatos ha de nombrar alcalde en Salasaca. Aug. 28. Legajos IV, ACA.

Saroli, Anna

2005 The Persistence of Memory: Traditional Andean Culture Expressed in Recurrent Themes and Images in Quechua Love Songs. *Confluencia* 20(2):47–56.

Schechner, Richard

2002 *Performance Studies: An Introduction*. London and New York: Routledge.

Schwartz, Stuart B., and Frank Salomon

1999 New Peoples and New Kinds of People: Adaptation, Readjustment, and Ethnogenesis in South American Indigenous Societies (Colonial Era). In *The Cambridge History of Native Peoples of the Americas*, ed. Frank Salomon and Stuart B. Schwartz, 443–501. Vol. 3, *South America*, part 2. Cambridge: Cambridge University Press.

Silverblatt, Irene

1987 *Moon, Sun, and Witches: Gender Ideologies and Class in Inca and Colonial Peru*. Princeton, N.J.: Princeton University Press.

Starn, Orin

1991 Missing the Revolution: Anthropologists and the War in Peru. *Cultural Anthropology* 6:63–91.

1994 Rethinking the Politics of Anthropology: The Case of the Andes. *Current Anthropology* 35(1):13–38.

Stromberg, Peter

1981 Consensus and Variation in the Interpretation of Religious Symbolism: A Swedish Example. *American Ethnologist* 8(3):544–59.

Sutton-Smith, Brian

1997 *The Ambiguity of Play*. Cambridge, Mass.: Harvard University Press.

Taussig, Michael

1987 *Shamanism, Colonialism, and the Wildman: A Study in Terror and Healing*. Chicago: University of Chicago Press.

1993 *Mimesis and Alterity: A Particular History of the Senses*. New York: Routledge.

Taylor, Lawrence J.

1995 *Occasions of Faith: An Anthropology of Irish Catholics*. Philadelphia: University of Pennsylvania Press.

Taylor, William

1996 *Magistrates of the Sacred: Priests and Parishioners in Eighteenth-Century Mexico*. Stanford: Stanford University Press.

Tedlock, Barbara

1991 The Emergence of Narrative Ethnography. *Journal of Anthropological Research* 47:69–94.

Tilley, Christopher Y.

1994 A Phenomenology of Landscape: Places, Paths, and Monuments. Oxford and Providence, R.I.: Berg.

Townsend, Joan B.

1997 Shamanism. In Anthropology of Religion: A Handbook, ed. Stephen D. Glazier, 429–69. Westport, Conn.: Praeger.

Tuan, Yi-fu

1977 Space and Place: The Perspective of Experience. Minneapolis: University of Minnesota Press.

Turino, Thomas

1983 The Charango and the "Sirena": Music, Magic, and the Power of Love. Latin American Music Review 4(1):81–119.

1993 Moving away from Silence: Music of the Peruvian Altiplano and the Experience of Urban Migration. Chicago: University of Chicago Press.

Turner, Victor

1979 Process, Performance, and Pilgrimage: A Study in Comparative Symbology. New Delhi: Concept.

Tylor, Edward B.

1965 [1873] Animism. In Reader in Comparative Religion: An Anthropological Approach, ed. William A. Lessa and Evon Z. Vogt, 10–21. 2nd ed. New York: Harper and Row.

Ulloa, Antonio de

1772 A Voyage to South America. Vol. 1. London: Gale Group Eighteenth-Century Collections Online.http://galenet.galegroup.com.

Urton, Gary

1980 Celestial Crosses: The Cruciform in Quechua Astronomy. Journal of Latin American Lore 6(1):87–110.

Uzendoski, Michael

2005 The Napo Runa of Amazonian Ecuador. Urbana: University of Illinois Press.

Vecinos de Salasaca al Arzobispo

1914 Los vecinos del caserío de Salasaca al Arzobispo sobre el cura Doctor Luis Fernando Bucheli. Jan. 12, Legajos IV, ACA.

Velasco, Juan de

1998 [1788] Historia del Reino de Quito en la América Meridional. Vol. 3, part 1. Quito: Casa de la Cultura Ecuatoriana.

Villalba, Jorge, SJ

2001 La primera evangelización del Reino de Quito. In Historia de la Iglesia Católica en el Ecuador. Vol. 1, ed. J. S. Lara, 127–54. Quito: Abya-Yala.

Waskosky, Kristine

1992   Affixes of Salasaca Quichua with Special Attention to Derivational Affixes Which Attach to Verbs. MA thesis. Grand Forks, University of North Dakota.

Weismantel, Mary

1988   *Food, Gender, and Poverty in the Ecuadorian Andes.* Philadelphia: University of Pennsylvania Press.

2001   *Cholas and Pishtacos: Stories of Race and Sex in the Andes.* Chicago: University of Chicago Press.

Whitten, Dorothea S.

2003   Actors and Artists from Amazonia and the Andes. In *Millennial Ecuador: Critical Essays on Cultural Transformations and Social Dynamics,* ed. Norman E. Whitten Jr., 242–74. Iowa City: University of Iowa Press.

Whitten, Dorothea S., and Norman E. Whitten Jr.

1988   *From Myth to Creation.* Urbana and Chicago: University of Illinois Press.

Whitten, Norman E. Jr.

1976   *Sacha Runa: Ethnicity and Adaptation of Ecuadorian Jungle Quichua.* Urbana: University of Illinois Press.

1985   *Sicuanga Runa: The Other Side of Development in Amazonian Ecuador.* Urbana: University of Illinois Press.

2003   Introduction to *Millennial Ecuador: Critical Essays on Cultural Transformations and Social Dynamics,* ed. Norman E. Whitten, 1–45. Iowa City: University of Iowa Press.

Whitten, Norman E., Dorothea S. Whitten, and Alfonso Chango

1997   Return of the Yumbo: The Indigenous Caminata from Amazonia to Andean Quito. *American Ethnologist* 24(2):355–91.

Wibbelsman, Michelle

2009   *Ritual Encounters: Otavalan Modern and Mythic Community.* Urbana: University of Illinois Press.

Williams, Derek

2005   The Making of Ecuador's Pueblo Católico, 1861–1875. In *Political Cultures in the Andes 1750–1950,* ed. Nils Jacobsen and Cristóbal Aljovín de Losada, 207–29. Durham, N.C., and London: Duke University Press.

Winkelman, Michael

1997   Altered States of Consciousness and Religious Behavior. In *Anthropology of Religion: A Handbook,* ed. Stephen D. Glazier, 394–428. Westport, Conn.: Praeger.

Wogan, Peter

2004   *Magical Writing in Salasaca: Literacy and Power in Highland Ecuador.* Boulder, Colo.: Westview Press.

Index

About the Author

Rachel Corr is associate professor of anthropology at the Wilkes Honors College of Florida Atlantic University. She received her PhD in anthropology from the University of Illinois at Urbana-Champaign. She has been undertaking research on Salasacan ritual and social life since 1990 and has published articles in the journals *Food and Foodways*, *Ethnology*, and *Journal of Latin American and Caribbean Anthropology*. She has also contributed a chapter to *Millennial Ecuador: Critical Essays on Cultural Transformations and Social Dynamics*, edited by Norman E. Whitten Jr (University of Iowa Press, 2003). She continues to study ritual and history in the context of North Andean ethnohistory. Her current research project focuses on ethnogenesis and cultural change in colonial Ambato, Ecuador.